DECADES

Alice Cooper

in the 1970s

Chris Sutton

sonicbondpublishing.com

Sonicbond Publishing Limited
www.sonicbondpublishing.co.uk
Email: info@sonicbondpublishing.co.uk

First Published in the United Kingdom 2021
First Published in the United States 2021

British Library Cataloguing in Publication Data:
A Catalogue record for this book is available from the British Library

Copyright Chris Sutton 2021

ISBN 978-1-78952-104-7

Typeset in ITC Garamond & ITC Avant Garde
Printed and bound in England

Graphic design and typesetting: Full Moon Media

Dedications and Thanks

Dedicated to Jacqui Sutton, Phil McMullen
and Charlie Millward

Special thanks to Michael Bruce,
Dennis Dunaway and Neal Smith

Also to Ernie Cefalu, Prakash John, Mick Mashbir,
Allan Schwartzberg and John Tropea

Author's Note

As well as my own thoughts on the music, it was important to me to get new content and perspective from those who were there at the time the music was recorded or performed. To this end, I made a list of everybody who had been involved – musicians, recording staff, band insiders, promoters etc. – and contacted as many as I could. Those who responded are listed below. In particular, those I have already thanked were more generous with their time than I could ever have hoped for.

Two things are worth noting. Firstly, both the pride in their work and the eagerness to help me by Dennis, Michael and Neal were utterly overwhelming. Secondly, the musicians from Alice's early solo years had, for the most part, never been asked about their work. Several went back to listen again to the albums before, after, and sometimes even during, our chats. They all enjoyed reconnecting again with the records and were pleased to be part of the legacy. All of the quotes you will see in this book are from those dozens of chats, all conducted in 2020 unless otherwise noted.

I have taken a little poetic licence in including 1969 in our story. Every great banquet has a starter and it felt right to include that year as it's an important starting point in our tale.

This book is a celebration of the music of Alice Cooper, and, while we won't agree on everything, I hope it inspires you to get the records out again and hear some things you might have missed. It's for all of you Sick Things everywhere.

Author Interviews & Correspondence

Mike Allen, Johnny Badanjek, Robin Black, Joe Bouchard, Michael Bruce, Janice Buxton-Davison, Ernie Cefalu, Bill Champlin, Cindy Dunaway, Dennis Dunaway, Dave Fisher, Jay Graydon, Jake Hawkins, Steve Hunter, Prakash John, Dave Libert, Fred Mandel, Peter Martin, Mick Mashbir, Jim Mason, Jonny Podell, Allan Schwartzberg, Neal Smith, John Tropea, Reggie Vincent, Ernie Watts

DECADES | Alice Cooper in the 1970s

Contents

Back To School

When the lights came up, it was a moment that many of us in the crowd had waited most of our lives to see. There on-stage at Birmingham Genting Arena (the N.E.C. to old-timers) was Alice Cooper playing a mini-set after he had finished his main set. Alongside him, at long last, were his former compadres – Michael Bruce, Dennis Dunaway and Neal Smith, with Ryan Roxie deputising for the sadly departed Glen Buxton. Birmingham was one of their first gigs in the UK since the four concerts they last played here in 1971/72. The atmosphere was highly charged and emotional.

The importance of the songs that Alice (collectively and solo) recorded in the 1970s was there to be seen in the set-list for that 2017 'Spend The Night With Alice Cooper' UK tour. Out of the twenty-two song set, thirteen were from the 1970s.

Over the subsequent decades, it's the 1970s recordings that have been the mainstay of his set-lists and remain the enduring musical legacy of Alice Cooper. There have been fine albums and wonderful songs by Alice since then, but it's the 70s which saw Alice Cooper established as a musical force, first as a group and then as a solo artist.

Like their biggest hit it all began back in school – Cortez High School in Phoenix, Arizona. Vincent Furnier, school newspaper (The Tip Sheet) columnist and track athlete volunteered to organise the Spring 1964 Lettermen Talent Show. Appearing on the bill were The Earwigs, who formed especially for the occasion but mostly had a singular lack of ability to play. The band were Vince himself on vocals and guitar, Dennis Dunaway – guitar, Glen Buxton – guitar, John Speer – guitar, and Phil Wheeler – snare drum. They dressed like the Beatles and performed covers of 'Please Please Me' and 'She Loves You 'with revised track lyrics and, similarly, The Flares' song 'Foot Stompin''. Wheeler left after this show, so John Speer replaced him on drums, with John Tatum coming in on second guitar. The new line-up got down to practising, rehearsing and playing gigs at Cortez.

Glen's sister Janice recalls Glen's early influences: 'My brother Ken loved jazz. When we moved to Arizona Ken stayed in Akron to finish his senior year. We took his record player and records in the move. Because we knew we weren't supposed to touch his stuff, Glen and I were all over it. Glen used to listen to the Dave Brubeck album, with Blue Rondo a la Turk, that's where his love of jazz came from. Of course, he listened to Chuck Berry, and 'Guitar Boogie'. He loved Duane Eddy's twangy sound and he also liked the Yardbirds a lot.'

Glen gave Dennis lessons on the bass as he picked up his distinctive style. Vince became lead vocalist, picking up tambourine or harmonica when needed. Janice: 'They began practising in our garage, which wasn't ideal. A garage band in Phoenix in the summer, that's dedication. The temperature then is about 105 degrees up'. The efforts over that hot summer of '65 paid off when The Earwigs got an audition for Jack Curtis, a local promoter, and owner of the V.I.P. Club. Curtis liked the band and decided to put them on regularly, but wasn't so keen on the band name. So the Earwigs morphed into The Spiders. The band specialised in cover versions, with the Rolling Stones, and particularly the Yardbirds, being firm favourites. The Spiders were a raucous attitude driven band, already looking at stage presentation and trying out different ideas. Dressed in black and performing with a large spider web (made of rope) they cut a different vibe to other bands in the area.

September 1965 saw two major events for The Spiders. On the 4th they supported The Yardbirds at the V.I.P. – about as good as it gets for huge Yardbirds fans. Topping that was the recording of a single for Curtis. 'Why Don't You Love Me', backed with 'Hitch Hike', was released on Curtis's Mascot Records label. The A-side was originally recorded by Merseybeat band The Blackwells, which The Spiders would have seen them play in the film *Ferry Cross The Mersey*, released earlier that year. Their version is a close facsimile of this energetic R 'N' B song. 'Hitch Hike' was originally written and performed by Marvin Gaye, but the band chose to go with the arrangement The Rolling Stones came up with for their *Out Of Our Heads* album. It suits them well, with Vince aping Mick Jagger's delivery and Glen playing an effective guitar solo.

Mike Ellen joined the band in 1966 as their roadie. 'I got the job through Glen. We became friends while in college. He was particularly fond of Chet Atkins and he owned a Gretsch guitar like the one Atkins played. Actually, my car got the job. I was driving a big piece of American steel, a Plymouth station wagon complete with rear fins. It could seat nine comfortably, so I started hauling their equipment. I received the nickname of 'Amp Boy' by the group.'

Summer 1966 saw John Tatum leave the band, to be replaced by Michael Bruce. Michael:

I got a call from a buddy who told me that John Tatum had left the band. He had a habit when they were playing as The Spiders at the V.I.P. They would have just finished a Yardbirds song; next song would be

'Satisfaction' by The Rolling Stones, John would go "da da dad da dahhh" on his guitar before the song started, just to show off. He was an arrogant guy. I was working at the time with Bill Spooner in a band called Our Gang. John Tatum wanted to be in a different band so he could let his ego creep, but Bill Spooner had an ego to match, if not greater than, John Tatum.

Michael joining The Spiders was sealed by his musicianship, and also his transport. 'I had a Willeys jeep, a 1950's one, which had wood on the floors and side, so I could carry some gear'.Meanwhile, Tatum hooked up with Spooner, meaning that Our Gang and The Spiders had swapped guitarists! But, as Michael recalls, things didn't work out for Tatum. 'The band lasted about a month and John came looking for his job back, and we said, 'No way'.'

Michael was a huge asset to The Spiders; he sang, played guitar and wrote. He had recorded a single with his band Wild Flowers in 1966 called 'A Man Like Myself'/'On A Day Like Today'. On second guitar in Wild Flowers was Mick Mashbir, who returns to the Alice Cooper story a few years later.

In September The Spiders released their second single (on Santa Cruz Records), recorded at Copper State Studios in Tucson, with Forster Cayce handling engineering duties. Michael's suggestion that the band should write their own material inspired Dennis and Vince, who came up with the A-side – 'Don't Blow Your Mind'. Mike Ellen: 'He (Cayce) tried to tell the band how the song should be produced by referring to The Fortunes song 'You Got Your Troubles' – It was way over my eighteen-year-old head!' The song, with a heavy Yardbirds influence, is a lost psych classic. It features the first great Dennis bass line, which drives the song along. Michael's presence on second guitar was a major boost in the rhythm sound too. Over it all Glen plays a wild fuzz pedalled lead guitar, adding to the excitement Vince puts across in the vocals. The B-side was 'No Price Tag', written by Vince and Glen. It's a less impressive derivative song in the style of The Rolling Stones.

The Spiders briefly 'returned' in 1998 when Sundazed Records issued a 7" EP of their two A-sides plus 'Hitch Hike' and an instrumental take of 'Why Don't You Love Me'.

There was a limit to how far you could progress in Phoenix, so the band moved to Los Angeles in spring 1967. A new name was also the order of the day with The Spiders becoming The Nazz, inspired by a Yardbirds song called 'The Nazz Are Blue'. The 'new band' recorded a single, for Very Records, called 'Wonder Who's Loving Her Now?' backed with 'Lay Down And Die, Goodbye'. Mike Ellen:

> They were produced by Dick Phillips (later known as Dick Christian), who was the group's road manager and a friend. It was an attempt to make a commercial record that would be played on top 40 radio. 'Lay Down And Die' was Glen's guitar tribute to The Yardbirds. I believe Mike Bruce wrote 'Wonder Who's Loving Her Now'. It was his style back then, but it still would have been a collaborative effort.

The A-side is an aching groove to lost love with a haunting melody. It fits in with that summer of '67 vibe and paves the way towards *Pretties For You,* which it would have seamlessly fitted in on, as would the B-side. 'Lay Down' was later re-worked for *Easy Action,* but this version is concise and far better. A whole album of this kind of material by The Nazz would have been fascinating. Both songs were credited to the whole band, including Speer, who left, or was sacked, in December. Michael recalls the difficulties with Speer: 'He had this amazingly hot temper. You'd say it's black and he'd say it's white'. His replacement was Neal Smith, a close friend of the band who had been stopping with them. Neal:

> Glen was the reason I got into the band. We went to college together and became friends. I was in art classes with Glen, some with Den and some with Alice. Once Glen and I realised we were both from Akron, Ohio, we instantly bonded.

The band had an unusual rehearsal space they liked to use at the time. Neal:

> We would go out to the desert in Arizona to one of the parks and the pavilion at night. We would set up an amplifier, one snare drum, and I think I had a cymbal, and it was amazing how we just locked in. Some of those jams became songs on *Pretties For You* and *Easy Action.* But more than anything we were learning about our relationship as a rhythm section. The chemistry just gelled better once I was there. I really understood what they were doing.

The vibe of The Nazz's single carried over into another 1967 release; Wild Flowers released 'More Than Me'/'Moving Along With The Sun', both tracks featuring a certain Bruce Michael. This was his attempt to separate the project from The Nazz with some anonymity! 'Moving Along With The Sun' in particular is terrific, reminiscent of The Mamas and The Papas.

In December '67, soon after Neal joined, the band auditioned for Mercury Recording Studio in Hollywood L.A. According to Dennis, they were offered a deal if they replaced Vince! But, as Neal stresses, it was a case of all for one. 'We said no, and that's how tight the band was. We were going to make it as a unit'. It was the right decision, but it has a certain irony later on in their career.

The emergence of Todd Rundgren's band, also called The Nazz, was the catalyst for the final name change. Dennis told *Goldmine* in 2019 that:

> Alice said, 'Alice Cooper. It's like Lizzie Borden, it's like the innocent little girl with a hatchet behind her back' and we're like, 'I don't know if we're ready for that'. That night I went home and my parents asked, 'What are you up to?' I told them, 'We're coming up with a new name for the band'. They asked me what I had come up with and I said 'Alice Cooper', and the expression on their faces sold me. They were in shock, and so then the next night I went back and now Alice had me on his side, and we both talked the rest of the guys into it, but only as a band name not as Alice's name, that was the name of all five of us.

It's a considerably less dramatic story than that given to the press, and still presented on occasion to this day, that the name came from a session with an Ouija board, which yielded the revelation that Vince Furnier had been a witch named Alice Cooper. Maybe the two stories are connected!

The first gig as Alice Cooper took place at Earl Warren Fairgrounds in Santa Barbara on 16 March 1968. Posters for the show billed them as The Nazz, but this was changed just before the show. Also changed was Vince's name – he too became known as Alice Cooper. This eventually led to him becoming the chief focus for publicity and promotion but, as Neal points out, 'In the inner circle we were all 20% of the same team. Everybody in that band did their part to make Alice Cooper a household name.'

Two days later the band were taken on as the house support band at the 20,000 capacity Cheetah Ballroom in Venice Beach. Mike Ellen: 'Sherry Cottle, the manager, liked them and they worked there quite often. She also got them other jobs. This is where they got into their psychedelic phase with clothing and a bit of theatre'.

In spite of the encouraging signs, the band were still running on a tight budget with little sustenance. Neal: We were trying to make enough money to buy beer and food. Believe me in that order too!' Glen told *Just Testing* in 1996: 'Usually the tightest a band ever is, is when they're starving to death. You know like sure I'll help you carry your bass amp up like nine flights of stairs, no problem. Then when you make it, £5,000 a week, it's pick up your own, do it yourself. I've had enough of your guff'. Things picked up when Neal's sister Cindy joined the band in Hollywood and got a job at the Inside Outside boutique, using her earnings to buy food for the band. She was a major asset in keeping them going. Neal:

She was with us when we went to Europe. She was at our house in Hollywood Hills and took care of the band. She had $50 a week to feed eight people and she did it. At least by that time, we had some money, before that we had no money. She took care of the house, as she did when we went to Pontiac, and at the mansion in Greenwich. She was always making clothes for us. Back when we were in California, she would go to the movie companies' sales where they got rid of their old wardrobes. She found all these amazing clothes and that's where some of the clothes came from on the album sleeves. They sold the clothes by the pound weight – a dollar a pound. I had a coat that Yul Brynner wore in The King And I, and a Spanish bolero vest I still have from an Abbot and Costello movie.

On 12 July the band auditioned for Frank Zappa. The eager group famously turned up for their 6:30 pm appointment at 6.30 am. Awakened by the group sound-checking Zappa came down and heard them play and was intrigued. Michael: 'We played "10 Minutes Before The Worm", "B. B. On Mars" and "Lay Down And Die, Goodbye". He gave us a compliment; "you guys can speed up or slow down like you are turning the voltage control on a motor". We rehearsed a lot at that'. They possibly played a fourth song for Zappa, who decided they were worth picking up and offered them a contract. Before the band went to sign, an opportune meeting took place. While working at the store, Cindy met Shep Gordon and Joe Greenberg, who purported to be the West Coast management for The Left Banke. She suggested the duo meet the Coopers, who were still managerless. They hit it off, and Shep and Joe became their managers on a handshake; no formal contract was signed or ever has been. Meanwhile, Zappa and his manager Herb Cohen were also looking at taking on the Alice Cooper management, so it was an unwelcome surprise to them when the previously unmentioned Shep and Joe turned up to go over the recording contract with Zappa's label, Straight Records.

Other positive news came with Dennis and Cindy telling the rest of the band they were now an item. Dennis: 'There was a time we were tiptoeing around, wondering if it would affect the dynamics of the band. Finally, we broke the news'. Neal still glows at the memory: 'It's amazing how it worked out with her and Dennis. It made the band even more of a family'.

The first time Zappa, Shep and Joe saw the band play live was the infamous gig at The Cheetah Club on 14 July. As well as the audience in the club, there was a crowd on the beach who were able to hear the music. Unfortunately, the group had sound and equipment problems, and their increasingly wayward performance saw people leaving in droves. By the end, there were only a few people left, but Shep was amazed at the intensity of the reaction, which, he reasoned, could be turned around to something positive. Joe, meanwhile, promised they would get better equipment, while Zappa put them on the bill for a forthcoming show. He still needed to see and hear them properly. That gig was on 23 July supporting Zappa And The Mothers Of Invention at the Whisky A Go Go in Los Angeles. Later the band went round to Zappa's house to listen to the tapes of their performance and were given the thumbs up to record an album. The (short) sessions for that album took place in November. 1969 was to be the year that Alice Cooper started to make a noise on record as well as at gigs; a year they started to make their mark.

1969: Painting A Picture To Show Everyone In The World

A notable start to the year was their residency supporting Led Zeppelin at the Whisky A Go Go from 2 to 5 January. The same month saw bizarre scenes at another gig. Michael:

> We opened for Steppenwolf at the University of Colorado, Boulder, an outdoor concert. We were playing 'Don't Blow Your Mind' and then we go into the middle section – what you see on the Toronto footage. Alice leaps off the stage and now he's running round the track. Not racing anybody, just running round the track and people start getting up and cheering him and he's coming round the corner, jumps back on stage grabs the mic and we go right back into the end of 'Don't Blow Your Mind'. The crowd went crazy and after our show, people were leaving. That was mind-blowing for us.

The band's truck and equipment were stolen in late January, but the band turned it into a positive, taking the mini enforced lay-off as an opportunity to get new stage clothes and props. Their gig at the Avalon Ballroom, San Francisco on 30 March gives a good idea of how the band sounded live at this time. It was given a semi-official release as the bonus selections on the *Nobody Likes Us* CD. A typical set from the dates supporting *Pretties For You* would be: 'No Longer Umpire', 'Reflected', '10 Minutes Before The Worm', 'Sing Low Sweet Cheerio', 'B. B. On Mars', 'Fields Of Regret', 'Nobody Likes Me' and 'Animal Pajamas'. Three other songs – 'Today Mueller', 'Levity Ball' and 'Changing Arranging' – had all been in the set in 1968 and were possibly featured on some dates in 1969 too.

Billboard reported in April on the launch of Zappa's Straight Records. Due up first was the release of 'Reflected' as a single, followed by the album *Pretties For You* shortly after that. The album, though, was delayed until the end of June. The band went back on the road to promote their records, with Jonny Podell joining their growing organisation as the band's booking agent, a job that would get both easier and harder as their reputation grew.

The show at Arizona Veterans Memorial Coliseum on 23 May was memorable for Janice Buxton. 'I saw them for the first time without my parents at the Coliseum with Iron Butterfly. It was fabulous! They made me popular at school. I learned pretty quickly about people who want to be your friend because of the band'.

By now the band felt Los Angeles was not getting what they were about; the dilemma was where they should relocate. The Saugatuck Pop Festival in Michigan on 4 to 5 July helped them with the decision. The stage was attacked by a wild crowd and declared unsafe, leaving the band to abandon the show. Alice described it to the *Detroit News* in 2008 as a light-bulb moment: 'I said, This is our audience right here! Where L.A. didn't get it, Detroit totally got it'. Detroit was to become their new home.

If the band had played the legendary Woodstock Festival in August, there is no doubt they would have got headlines, but the band felt they hadn't missed out. Michael: 'Woodstock was yesterday's music and we were at the front of what was to come, you know?' It was ironic then that they got the headlines because of their appearance on 13 September at the 'Rock 'N' Roll Revival' festival at the Varsity Stadium in Toronto. The stellar bill included Chuck Berry, Jerry Lee Lewis, Gene Vincent, Little Richard, Junior Walker and Bo Diddley from the 'old guard' plus The Doors and a début appearance by John Lennon and the Plastic Ono Band. How did the Coopers manage to get on such a stellar bill? Dennis: 'The festival promoter wanted John Lennon to do it, but it got beyond his capabilities, so Joe and Shep said they would help him pull off the festival, but the deal would be Alice Cooper gets to be on the bill'. In addition, it was agreed that the band would back Gene Vincent for his performance, for which they were called The Vagabond Motorbike Gang. The band's own set was a barnstorming display of visceral power which has survived in great quality on film and audio (*Nobody Likes Us*).

The headlines came because Toronto was the scene of the chicken incident when Alice threw one into the audience, thinking it could fly. How it got on stage at all isn't certain, but what is certain is that the audience pulled it apart and threw the remains back at the stage. Dennis:

Right after the chicken thing, everybody was freaking out, why are these guys on the rock 'n' roll bill anyway? The whole stadium went quiet. We were supposed to go and change and come on later, but they said to get him (Gene Vincent) out there so people can see why they're on the bill. They forced him to come out when we were covered in sweat and feathers, and stuff all over the stage. He was in shock. I remember him walking out and seeing us for the first time in our outfits and everything, because when we rehearsed we just had t-shirts and jeans and blue caps. I think we pulled it off, but it was just so anti-climactic after what had just happened. Alice probably played tambourine or maracas, something like that. He stayed out there too.

Sadly there seems to be no record, not even a photograph, of their performance with Gene Vincent.

However, the drama was not yet over in Toronto for the band. Dennis:

There was a club there called the Rock Pile. The guy knew the festival was going to wipe out his business, so he made an announcement that after the festival anyone could bring their sleeping bags and crash there, and there would be mellow music all night. Well, the guy thought that Alice Cooper sounded like normal music, so he hired us and when we came walking in he was like, 'Oh no!', but we promised we would tone it down. We went on at four in the morning. People were asleep and we gave it the full show, the feathers and everything. The guy said he wasn't going to pay us. Then Joe and Shep told him, 'You want everyone to think you are the hippest club in Toronto, wait till word gets out that you thought Alice Cooper was a girl folk singer'. They not only talked him into paying us; they talked him into giving us another gig a couple of weeks later. When we came back, there were still feathers stuck in the corners of the room.

The following night they were in Toledo, Ohio, on a bill that included Detroit friends The Amboy Dukes, The Frost (with Dick Wagner) and the MC5. On what was a particularly wild night Glen Buxton was stretchered off stage after being hit in the knee by a flying hammer.

When they supported the Who on 11 October at The Grande-Riviera Ballroom in Detroit, they had a special guest star almost appear. Neal:

After the show, 'Goose', my drum roadie, told me that during our last song (probably 'Animal Pajamas'), Keith Moon was playing drums along with me. Behind me was a giant movie screen separating the Who's equipment and ours. The screen was transparent from behind so Keith could see me through the screen, but from the front with lights shining on it, you could see Keith playing along with me.

What a mouth-watering combination, Neal Smith and Keith Moon playing together!

Sometime in the Fall, the band recorded a cameo appearance for the film *Diary Of A Mad Housewife*. You don't see much of them in the party-scene sequence, but you can hear them throughout it. The producers wanted Steppenwolf but couldn't get them, so the Coopers obliged by playing a Mars Bonfire (of Steppenwolf) song, 'Ride With Me' from his début solo album. After running through that, they launched into 'Lay Down And Die, Goodbye'.

Surprisingly a new contract was signed with Straight in October. It was an extension for two more albums to be completed by 1 May 1970. There would then be the option of an extra year should they achieve sales of 150,000 copies or more of these two albums. What this meant in the short term was that the band had just over a month to complete *Easy Action*. This then gave them six more months in which to turn round what would become *Love It To Death* by the deadline. Additionally, the band secured a songwriters' deal with Straight, who also agreed to pay 6,000 dollars a year to the band for being on their roster on top of the royalties.

Pretties For You (Straight)

Personnel:
Alice Cooper: lead vocals
Glen Buxton: lead guitar
Michael Bruce: rhythm guitar, keyboards, backing vocals, lead vocals on 'Living' and 'Sing Low Sweet Cheerio'
Dennis Dunaway: bass, backing vocals
Neal Smith: percussion, backing vocals
Produced at Whitney Studios, Los Angeles, November 1968 by Frank Zappa and Ian Underwood.
USA release date: 25 June 1969. UK release date: June 1969
Highest chart places: USA: 194, UK: -
Running time: 38:10
All songs credited to Alice Cooper (group)

The most 'different' album they ever made; if this was by a still obscure band, it would be rightly hailed as a psychedelic classic. The temptation is to judge it against the later glories, but it's better judged on its own merits. Musically it covers a bewildering range of styles and time signatures, often in the same song!

There were tremendous issues at the recording sessions, none of which were down to the group who were just pleased to be making an album.

The producer, Frank Zappa himself, left the studio feeling ill partway through the first day of recordings. Dennis:

> We (me and Cindy) were in the control room talking to him and he was complaining that he didn't feel good. Ian Underwood who came in and helped us with damage control, said, 'Believe me Frank is a musical workaholic, the only time he doesn't show up is if he is really sick. He's not bailing on you.'

Shep claimed that when Zappa returned, later that day, he told them that the album was finished. Dennis: 'Several of those songs we didn't even know Frank was recording. We were just running through the songs to warm up. He said OK we got some takes here. We told him we hadn't known he was recording us yet and there were mistakes. But he just said, 'We can fix it in the mix'. Fortunately Ian Underwood said, 'I'll help you guys'. We didn't know how to work the equipment or anything'. Underwood was the Mothers Of Invention's keyboardist, and without him, the album would not have been completed, but fundamentally this crucial début was made up, save a few overdubs, of a rehearsal recording.

The cover, actually titled *Pretties For You,* was painted by Ed Beardsley. The concept of the painting was the dreams and regrets of an old man as death approaches. A striking, surreal image that feels like a reasonable fit for the music inside. It ran into trouble with the censors due to the young lady displaying her 'pretties', so early copies had a sticker to cover her modesty. The painting was purchased by Zappa and proudly displayed in his house. It wasn't the first choice for the cover – that was a Salvador Dali painting called 'Geopoliticus Child Watching The Birth Of The New Man', but the band couldn't get permission to use it. You can see the Dali painting on the 1975 album *Newborn* by The James Gang.

Zappa's involvement with them may have been brief, but he established a connection with Glen, who told *Just Testing* in a 1996 video interview that, 'He liked my guitar playing a lot. He had me play on a couple of his things, a couple of the projects he had going, so that was the biggest compliment I think I've ever had in my life'. What these projects were, remains a tantalising mystery.

'Titanic Overture'
Dennis: 'Michael decided we needed one more song and Morgan Studios in Burbank had this massive organ, with all these pipes inside the

walls. Michael decided he's going to play 'Titanic Overture', which was something he had been noodling around with on piano'.

It's an attention-grabbing opener, written and performed entirely by Michael. His idea was to play something that could be a soundtrack for the sinking of the Titanic. It does conjure up the feel of faded stately grandeur. If not the Titanic then a spooky *Phantom Of The Opera* type atmosphere. Right at the end of the tune, Michael switches to piano; it sounds a promising new section but fades out just as it gets going. The track is a dramatic and effective start to the band's début album, albeit a solo instrumental.

'10 Minutes Before The Worm'

The early bird catches the worm they say, and this time the bird is ten minutes early! While there are no birds or worms featured, there are guinea pigs. Dennis: 'When Michael was done with 'Titanic Overture' the band decided it was really important to record our guinea pigs, Bert (who was the girl) and Ethyl (who was the guy), chewing lettuce'. This effect was added to form the intro for the track. Glen's skittish guitar parts harmonise briefly with the guinea pigs before the song starts properly. It's about a minute long of odd nursery rhyme style verses with no chorus. There's a brief instrumental break with Glen's lead guitar sounding like nothing on earth before the final verse, concluding with 'everything is standing still'. The only thing that sounds normal on this oddity is the guinea pigs!

On the *Whisky '69* live recording, Alice credits the song as being written by Dennis.

'Sing Low, Sweet Cheerio'

The first 'proper' song on the album opens with acoustic guitar chords from Michael, which he rhythmically punctuates with hand slaps. Neal and Dennis come in, followed by Glen with some mournful electric guitar licks that are amongst his best playing on the album. Michael then swaps to his electric and fills out the bottom of the sound. It's the first evidence on record of just what the group had in the engine room with Michael, Dennis and Neal forming a unique rhythm section that allowed Dennis and Neal room to take off in different directions.

At 1:30, there's some Morse code SOS-style guitar notes which cue nicely into the 'Help me' lyrics. Those notes come back a few more times. Alice plays the harmonica on the instrumental break, and it's here that the band's jazz influences show through for the first time.

Michael says that this is a solo composition by him, with himself on lead vocals and Alice harmonising.

'Today Mueller'

Michelle 'Toodie' Muller was a friend of the band and got this song (almost) named for herself. It has a nursery rhyme quality to it, and a similar feel to the non-album track 'Nobody Likes Me'. The chorus has an edgy weirdness to it with those high harmonies as Alice asks Toodie to, 'Give your notice of your leaving'.

There's not much to it musically with everything following the vocal melody closely. Michael's piano dominates with little guitar at all until about a minute in when Glen plays some quirky fills which add emphasis to the overall strangeness going on. That nursery rhyme feel is highlighted at 1:03 when Alice sings the 'Red Rover, Red Rover, pass under, pass over, pass through'. These lines are from the children's game called Red Rover, which is not dissimilar to British Bulldog.

It's one of those tracks you can listen to and get something from, but with more time and thought on the track-list it could have been replaced by something better.

'Living'

This is a very under-rated song, written (says Michael) by Michael and Alice. It would have made a good single A-side with some tidying up, as it's a little too busy at times. The melody and lyrics have a happy, warm feel and there's a lot to enjoy, especially the buzzing speaker-shaking solo from Glen. The lead vocals feature Michael and Alice harmonising almost Beatles-style.

There were problems with Dennis's equipment, so the intention was to overdub the bass later. Dennis laughs: 'The band got distracted when Michael came up with 'Titanic Overture', so I said 'OK, I will do my bass part after that'. Then we got distracted yet again with guinea pig overdubs for '10 Minutes Before The Worm', so in the end, we ran out of time and it doesn't have any bass, that's Glen's guitar'. Dennis laughs again as he summarises that 'We decided it was more important to record guinea pigs chomping lettuce for the beginning of '10 Minutes Before The Worm' than it was to do the bass on 'Living'.

The song was also released as the B-side to an edited 'Reflected' and features Glen's lead guitar much higher in the mix. The mono mix compresses the sound spectrum together and it doesn't work as well as the expansive stereo mix, apart from the lead guitar!

'Fields Of Regret'

Dennis:

> People loved the dark character; he's doing all these different
> characters – the little kid for 'Nobody Likes Me', then the guy that saw a
> ghost for 'Levity Ball'. That's the one where the few people that would
> stay to the end of our show would be shouting 'fields, fields'. If we
> didn't play 'Fields' they would have been upset. I said it was the most
> popular thing we had got going and we should do more songs like that.
> We shouldn't drop it until we had another song that has that character.
> Then I said we should do that character for the whole show because
> that's what's connecting. It took us a couple of years to be able to write
> well enough to write the songs to support that character.

Alice also loves this track, which still sounds great in spite of the murky
production. Dennis plays high up the neck, so his bubbling bass runs
sit out from the sound, and it's his best work on the album. At 2:44
the band lock into a rolling lurching rhythm before heading into the
spoken word section. The words here are mixed too low, but it's clear
that they have real significance. They are taken from a 13th-century
Gregorian chant called 'Dies Irae (Days Of Wrath)' ascribed to Thomas
of Celano. The actual words, which Alice varies slightly, are three verses
from the work and the translation runs: 'What horror must invade the
mind, when the approaching Judge shall find, and sift the deeds of all
mankind! Now death and nature with surprise, behold the trembling
sinners rise to meet the Judge's searching eyes. When the doomed can
no more flee, from the fires of misery, with the chosen call me.'
    While it all appears rather grim, there are verses of hope in the
original work.
    Straight out of that section, Glen turns in a buzzing solo that builds
and builds in intensity. One of the best he ever played for the band. You
almost expect to hear Alice say, 'On lead guitar, Glen Buxton' after it.
From there it's a one-minute outro with the big finish.

'No Longer Umpire'

A great little track. Despite the perplexing title, the lyrics seem self-
referential. 'We've been so caught up in the subject of personnel',
with the band 'painting a picture to show everyone in the world'. The
fading up intro is nice, the bass and drums grabbing your attention

right away and the track has a real snap and punch to it with a nice fat bass sound from Dennis. Pre-dating the urgencies of punk, everything they wanted to get across they do perfectly in just over two frantic minutes.

'Levity Ball'

Despite the speed that the album was recorded at, the band still found time for at least one key decision on the music. This being that they had a better, more other-worldly, version of this song already on tape from a rehearsal at The Cheetah Club. It is an extraordinarily compelling performance. The intro is unusual, a bouncing noise that comes fast right at you and seems to speed by, before repeating. Dennis:

> That is the perfect example of playing dynamics. You mute the strings to start and that's the whole band doing that dynamic. Glen played the 'diddly diddly' part. I think Neal was in on it too. He plays really loud on this and then brings it all down.

It's the most out-there psychedelic track on the album. At 1:44 there's a change of dynamics and a long powerful instrumental section of unison descending notes, with Glen wailing away over it. The breakdown comes at 3:35, and if you listen closely, you can hear strange vocals and a string section. This is bleed-through from what was originally on the tape before they recorded the song. This end section of the song has a spectral beauty to it with Alice's best vocals on the album, 'Then in came a cake all decorated in my name'. He gets such a forlorn quality in his vocal here. Neal plays the ticking clock motif as the time is up for their first Levity Ball.

The studio take finally emerged on the *Life And Crimes* box-set and is great, but the spectral quality of the live version is missing.

'B.B. On Mars'

B.B. being a ball bearing, which out on Mars would be really small. Literally far out! What has this got to do with the song? Nothing, but it does mean the title is more interesting than the song. To be fair, the intro is a cool hard riff before giving way to a surging mid section that can't seem to find anywhere to go. It picks up at 0:57 with a unison outro riff that increases in speed, but this is another track that shouldn't have made the running order.

'Reflected'

Neal's widely panned drum intro heralds a descending riff and melody line. It's quite a simple song after the intro, which is by far the best bit. There is also some great wah-wah guitar going on, with a terrific solo at 2:40. Sonically it's too harsh and bright, but with more time and better production, this could have been another stand-out track.

Still, there was enough in the track for it to be edited as a single. The promising intro was revisited in 1972 for 'Elected', taking the best parts of the track and refining them. The melody and the descending guitar parts were re-used, as were the pulsing high notes from Dennis, and Alice's diction in the first verse. It is an interesting example of how their later output was transformed by working with Bob Ezrin.

'Apple Bush'

Various band members have said that the *Goldfinger* soundtrack provided inspiration, and this is one track where you can see that. The rolling jazzy rhythm that opens the song and punctuates it has some similarities to 'Into Miami' from the soundtrack. The best thing about this song is the relaxed jazzy swing feel. There's a diversion at 1:44 for contrast, but it's a little jarring, though Alice does get to play a harmonica break on it! The return to the warm gentler feel of the track takes us up to the outro with some false stops.

This is a pleasant but lesser song, though by no means the worst on the album. The lyrics are taken from an old poem by Neal. Michael feels this is a rare example of a composition by himself, Neal and Glen.

'Earwigs To Eternity'

Earwigs being a reference to the band's original incarnation. There are interesting things going on in this brief track, but it makes for a confusing packed 1:20 of ideas. When it finishes, you are left wondering, what the hell was that about?! It also sounds more like a demo than many of the other tunes, even considering they all (bar one) have the same recording background. Another that could have done with being dropped from the running order.

'Changing Arranging'

The big finish to the album is in a similar vein to 'Fields Of Regret'. It even utilises a similar 'drunken' sounding instrumental section with buzzing guitar. The verses and choruses show promise, but they don't work with the instrumental sections, which means there are two different tracks in effect. On the plus side, there is a great melodic descending section from 2:41 with nice harmony vocals that could have been developed further into a big finish for the album. In the end, it all just fades out, making for a frustrating finish to the album.

Related Songs
'Animal Pajamas' (Cooper/Bruce/Buxton/Dunaway/Smith)
Only live versions exist of this 20-minute track, sometimes credited as 'Don't Blow Your Mind' or 'Science Fiction Thriller'. Dennis:

> That was in the Iron Butterfly 'In A Gadda Da Vida' days. Big long productions that would eventually get round to the recognisable riff. That was our version of doing that. If we had put more thought into it and had more rehearsal space and time to develop it, it probably would have gone more in the direction of 'Halo Of Flies', with more parts and variation.

It's an astounding piece of music and theatre even now. The riff is indeed taken from the old Spiders song 'Don't Blow Your Mind', but played in bone-crunching, slow, heavy rock style. The piece goes through many twists and turns, even featuring the future intro riff of 'Halo of Flies', a drum solo and the spoken intro from *The Prisoner* TV series. The sound of the future was now! Hear it best on *Nobody Likes Us*.

'Nobody Likes Me' (Cooper/Bruce/Buxton/Dunaway/Smith)
How this got left off the album is a mystery. Dennis's tongue in cheek response was that 'It's like 'Strawberry Fields' not being on *Sgt. Pepper!*' Neal observes that: 'There's not too many that fell through the cracks. Luckily we did record a good version of it'.

Its inclusion would have seen one or two of the weaker tracks taken off the album. There are two studio versions in existence – the longest, and best, turns up on the *Old School* box-set. The second version was given a limited release as a flexi-disc on the back of the *Killer* tour programme and was featured on the *Life And Crimes* box-set. The two versions are different from each other, but either are well worth seeking out. The dynamics in the music are incredible. The instrumental break with what sounds like a concertina is fun and dramatic and there is a killer moment when it stops and Alice – who is superb on this – comes back in. His voice spiralling down resigned and beaten for the 'Never call, never write' section, with the backing chorus of nay-sayers adding a call and response touch. It's a fantastic, fun piece of work. Michael:

> Musically that was mostly Dennis and I. He had a natural musical feel in a songwriter way. We'd used it live in the chamber of fire – a phone booth looking thing without the walls, and we lit it on fire and Alice was in there singing 'Nobody Likes Me'. But the best part was the night the fire marshal got up there with a fire extinguisher and put it out!

In the notes for *Life And Crimes* Alice says that 'Dennis had the idea for this. My idea was when we performed it live, I would sing it through a window. Every kid has this experience of not getting picked to play on a team and then having to watch through the bedroom window with envy while others kids played without you, thinking that nobody likes you. Groucho Marx loved this song'. Groucho certainly recognised a classic piece of theatre in song when he heard one!

'Wonder Who's Loving Her Now'

A very brief instrumental snippet from rehearsals is in circulation which sounds fuller and brighter than the version released by The Nazz. It would have worked well on the album, and for most listeners would have been a previously unknown song, but the overall intention was to use the newer material that was firing the band up.

Archive releases
Nobody Likes Us (CD)

The main attraction on this is the set from the 1969 Toronto Rock 'N' Roll Revival show which has been released in myriad versions over the years. It first appeared in 1982 and caused instant confusion with misnamed track titles and two songs ('Ain't That Just Like A Woman' and 'Goin' To The River') that weren't even by the band, these being by Ronnie Hawkins.

Putting all that to one side there is an essential album to be heard here and thankfully Applebush Records put out the definitive version in 2012. It's the only version that runs at the right speed and features the full set. Michael Bruce supplied the song title details and corrected the running order. It's an astonishing performance on the edited video footage on Youtube, but it's no less powerful without the visuals on CD.

The band deliver bravura performances of 'No Longer Umpire', 'Lay Down And Die Goodbye', 'Fields of Regret' and 'Nobody Likes Me' before the 20-minute extraordinary conclusion to the set, identified by Michael as being called 'Animal Pajamas'.

The bonus tracks are from The Avalon Ballroom in San Francisco on 30 March 1969. Sadly the quality is very poor with severe tape flutter.

The packaging for the release is thoughtful, the design and colours alluding to *Pretties For You,* and a selection of contemporary photographs in the fold-out digipack.

Live At The Whisky '69 (CD and vinyl)

Actually recorded on 23 July 1968 at The Whisky A Go Go in Los Angeles. The band played this show supporting Frank Zappa and The Mothers of Invention. Zappa recorded his set and the Coopers' set was also recorded for him to hear them in a live setting. The eight songs featured represent a strong performance, more than good enough to get them the deal to record an album. The irony is that it is better produced than *Pretties For You* because the mix itself is better.

Dennis: 'At least on that Whisky show we had some separation. They had Wally Heider, who had a mobile recording truck in L.A., which was cutting edge at the time. We knew they were gonna record the Mothers, but we didn't know they were recording us. Still, at least we were prepared to do the show and give it our all, not warming up in the studio.'

1970: You Can Come Along With Me

The band began the year with tour dates building up till *Easy Action* was released on 27 March. Sometime in this period, the band made their planned move to Detroit. It's also in this era that *Diary Of A Mad Housewife* was released.

A stand-out performance over summer was their appearance on 13 June at the Midsummer Rock Festival at Crosley Field, Cincinnati. Their set was partly filmed by Cincinnati WLWT-T and featured in their broadcast footage. 'Black Juju' was the new song in the set. Dennis: 'The band hadn't even rehearsed the song and we decided we were going to do it on a live broadcast on a major network. We were going to do this song without even having played it before'. Neal adds: We were still working out the ending of the song in the limo on the way to the concert!' The band are on great form and Alice doesn't even let a cake thrown from the audience into his face put him off.

The band's on-stage appearance continued to attract attention, thanks to the brilliance of Cindy Smith:

I've loved glitter and sparkles ever since I was a small child. I've always found them magical. Since I was very young, I've been inspired by the beautiful Busby Berkeley musicals and costumes designed by Orry-Kelly. I also find dramatic clothing, movie costumes, colours and beautiful fabrics inspiring. As a teen I would rummage through racks at thrift stores and Goodwill, searching for cool, vintage-looking clothes, dramatic and usually a bit sparkly. My mother sewed growing up and taught me to hand sew. I really learned to sew from my Aunt M., who I lived with at the farm in Ohio during the summer. I started altering patterns to make my own designs. As far as the AC costumes, that was easy. I listened to the music for inspiration and used the theme for the stage show as inspiration too. The guys were amazing and so easy to work with and truly willing to wear anything I made. After a while, I just tailored it to their personalities.

The set on 23 July at the Chicago Underground in Warren, Michigan was recorded. It's the only record of an *Easy Action* era live set and it sees the band toying with future ideas. The set was:- 'Sun Arise', 'Mr. and Misdemeanor', 'Fields Of Regret', 'I'm Eighteen', 'Levity Ball', 'Is It My Body'/'Going To The Graveyard', 'Nobody Likes Me' and 'Lay Down And Die, Goodbye'. Little confidence is apparent in *Easy Action* with the bulk of the set being *Pretties For You* era or from the forthcoming *Love It To Death*. 'I'm Eighteen' is the long jamming version that Bob Ezrin was to hear soon and 'Is It My Body' is the longer prototype.

Shep and Joe contacted Jack Richardson, of Nimbus 9 production company in Toronto, with a view to him producing the band. They liked his work with The Guess Who and thought he would be a good fit. Unfortunately, Richardson hated *Easy Action*. In fact, nobody at Nimbus 9 liked it, so junior employee Bob Ezrin was sent to meet the band and give them the brush-off. Ezrin, however, was intrigued on meeting the band and agreed to go and see them live. That epochal event took place at Max's Kansas City in New York on 8 September. Ezrin was hooked by the power of their performance and one song in particular. Michael: 'Bob heard the chorus as 'I'm edgy' instead of 'I'm Eighteen'. He was impressed by the way the crowd reacted to the whole band's persona. Our band was like a smorgasbord, something for everybody'. Ezrin saw the potential and agreed to produce their next album, his first production (with Jack Richardson acting as executive producer).

The band and Ezrin did pre-production for the album at their ranch in Pontiac, sculpting their playing and the new material. But Warners, who had picked up Straight Records, were still unconvinced after two poor-selling albums, so they wanted a single first. No pressure but it would have to be something special. Fortunately, it was a superb calling card from the rejuvenated band.

'I'm Eighteen 'was released on 11 November, initially on Straight. It started to sell as radio stations picked up hundreds of phone calls from fans (and the band) to play the song and went on to be an enormous hit. The green-light was duly given for the crucial third album, which the band recorded over November/December in RCA, Chicago.

Two intriguing concerts took place at Christmas (25 and 26 December) when Bob Ezrin joined the band on-stage (playing keyboards) at the Eastown Theatre in Detroit. The year was ending positively for the band, but their faithful roadie had reluctantly decided to leave. Mike Ellen:

I never thought of it as a job– just a way to see musical groups and meet girls. I always thought it would be temporary, well temporary lasted for over four years. I quit before they became famous. Not that I didn't think they would become famous, I knew they would. I was getting burned out. I would drive or fly the equipment, set it up, take it down and then repeat that process over and over again. It was too much lifting with too little sleep. My 23-year-old body was feeling abused and it was letting me know about it. That being said, it was the greatest experience of my life. I had been living a part of the rock and roll dream. What eighteen to 23-year-old male wouldn't want to do that?

Easy Action (Straight)

Personnel:
Alice Cooper: lead vocals
Glen Buxton: lead guitar
Michael Bruce: rhythm guitar, keyboards, backing vocals, lead vocals on 'Below Your Means' and 'Beautiful Flyaway'
Dennis Dunaway: bass, backing vocals
Neal Smith: percussion, backing vocals
with:
David Briggs: piano on Shoe Salesman
Produced at Sunwest Studios, Hollywood, 1969-1970 by David Briggs.
USA release date: 27 March 1970. UK release date: April 1970
Highest chart places: USA: -, UK: –
Running time: 34:13
All songs credited to Cooper/Bruce/Buxton/Dunaway/Smith

The sophomore album from the band is, for the most part, more conventional than their début. The lack of time to prepare material put them on the back foot straight away, and what we get is a band looking for identity and focus.

David Briggs produced the album, in essence, the first producer they had properly worked with. It's said he was not keen on the material, although he must have liked 'Shoe Salesman' as he plays piano on it! Take that song, 'Laughing At Me' and' Beautiful Flyaway' and you would have a typical production from David Briggs, who was known for his work with Neil Young. He gets those down well, but he hasn't got the touch for the heavier tracks.

The minimal preparation shows in some weaker songs. It also sounds like they are one track short with a couple of songs stretched out to compensate. 'Below Your Means' and 'Lay Down And Die, Goodbye' both could have benefited from editing.

Oddly Alice Cooper (the singer) misses out on a fair part of the album! He isn't on 'Beautiful Flyaway' and only sings back-ups (if at all) on 'Below Your Means'. He also isn't on most of 'Lay Down And Die' so it does make for a curious listening experience at times. Dennis: 'Even if Alice wasn't singing, he was always there doing something. In the early days when people heard Michael sing, they would say 'wow, you sound a lot like Alice'. The truth was that Alice was imitating Michael because Michael would come in with the song and sing it and Alice would imitate him'.

There are moments when you can see what is coming ahead in their career, and it has been pegged as a 'sleeper' great album in the Alice catalogue.

It was the last album to credit all the songs to the entire band. Future album credits are more specific, and to some extent lessen the sense of all five being equally involved. Glen was no doubt thinking of this era when he told *Just Testing* in 1996 what the band had:

Alice was the word man. He really could turn a phrase, as it were. I used to do the guitar licks and then Mike Bruce would come up with the chord changes, and Dennis, of course, the bass parts and Neal with the drumming. It worked out well, we really all did contribute to all the songs.

The backs-to-the-camera front cover image was suggested by Neal Smith. It kind of says Alice Cooper are back, but then you see a front view of the band on the back cover. A perverse reversal of album cover convention!

'Mr. And Misdemeanor'

Glen's sister Janice says that the titular duo were Alice and Glen. It's got a swaggering feel to it and you can hear the sound edging towards *Love It To Death* in the verses. Just after the one-minute mark the tempo changes and we get a playful interlude before Neal changes gears as only he can, Alice wails, and we go back into the main song structure. It's a good opening track, and the band clearly thought so too because it made it into their live set.

On a note of trivia, the song name-checks the first album, and, more unusually, Kenny Passarelli, a friend of the band who went on to play with Joe Walsh and on Alice's *From The Inside* album. What he thought about being linked in the same line as the gangster Lucky Luciano is unknown! Michael feels that this song would be an early Bruce/Cooper credit.

'Shoe Salesman'

A different style for the band here, this is almost a straight pop song, albeit with obscure lyrics. Our salesman doesn't seem to sell any shoes but can offer you a popsicle. The clue to the song's real theme is in the marks on our salesman's arms.

David Briggs plays a complementary piano part that gives the song an almost jaunty air. It's still all rather innocuous, with only Glen's lead guitar parts keeping things interesting. It's another should-be Bruce/Cooper credit says Michael.

Surprisingly it was released in America and Canada as a slightly edited single, backed with 'Return Of The Spiders'. Unsurprisingly it didn't trouble the charts.

'Still No Air'

A stinging intro riff gives way to a heavy doom/gloom section. It's reminiscent of the feel of 'Fields Of Regret', but the quite literal breakdown section where it sounds like the song is falling apart gives way to another killer riff at 1:11. It's here we get more glimpses of the dynamics coming on the next album. It's also our first sighting of the band's love of 'West Side Story' – 'When you're a Jet, you're a Jet all the way, from your first cigarette to your last dying day'. The Jets will return on the *School's Out* album, but on that occasion, they will be the 'opposition'. This section of the track is also where the title of the album gets a mention – Alice's classic sneer of 'Easy Action'.

The song looks both backwards and forwards musically and was written by Michael, Alice and Dennis. For me, it's one of the best tracks on the album.

'Below Your Means'

This is a brooding track, written by Michael, and similar, in some ways, to the forthcoming 'Desperado'. Michael sings it, but it sounds like Alice with him on the choruses. It takes off in a new direction with the riff at 2:08, which works well, sounding like it might end at around the 3:30 mark, but no. Rather than go for a crashing end, the song goes into a third section which is fundamentally an instrumental jam. It sounds bolted on, and although it's interesting to hear the band jam like this, and there's undeniably good stuff going on, it's way too long and the extra-long fadeout with the surprise crash back in is tiresome.

'Return Of The Spiders'

There is a real urgency and drive here that has been mostly lacking so far. It's a great side two opener, which might have been a better choice for side one's opening track. Neal Smith's powerful snare drum attack dominates, reminiscent of The Surfaris' song 'Wipeout', which Smith had loved playing from way back. It's a pure orgy of noise with jagged guitar fills and Alice in imperious form. The opening line of 'Stop, look and listen, there are hands that are gathered here' grabs your attention, coming on a rush of sound that gives this album an almighty lift. The slight let down is that the track doesn't seem to know where to go. There is a great breakdown section, where Alice brings it back with an exultant 'Woah Ohhhhhhh', but it just goes into a faded outro that is more of the same.

It was the only track from their first two albums to survive in the set-lists in the *Love It To Death* era shows. The band dedicated it to Gene Vincent, who they backed at the Toronto festival, with another nice touch being that reference to their first recording band, The Spiders.

'Laughing At Me'

Neal: 'That was an early commercial attempt, I don't know where it would have fit on a future album. It's a Michael Bruce song and you can tell, his song-writing was Beatle-esque, he really was a student of the Beatles'. Dennis is also a fan: 'I love that song. I like what Glen played and the moodiness of it'.

It's a great 'sleeper' track. Nobody singles it out, but it's one of the best tracks on the album, a real Alice Cooper gem, and a song that warrants more exposure. The lyrics are minimal, but Alice makes them count, giving this song a sad tone that is picked up in the music. There are some lovely chord changes and a loose groove that works a treat. The guitar solo is perfect light jazz and one of the best things on the whole album. Michael adds that Alice contributed some of the words too.

'Refrigerator Heaven'

The song was inspired by alleged reports that Walt Disney had been cryogenically preserved after his death in case he could be cured in the future. A great song idea.

An icy wind and distant cries (almost like an audience) open things up. The icy cold feel is maintained with 'ice cracking' guitar effects and insistent phased percussion. Even though it's under two minutes long, the band still find time for a change of pace and feel at 0:50, which is not dissimilar to the break during 'Mr. And Misdemeanor'. It's a good song, especially on the verses, and shows the way forward for the band.

Looking backwards, it name-checks 'B. B. On Mars' off *Pretties For You* in the lyrics, but the song also points to the band's future direction. The refrigerator setting would return again in Alice's nightmares.

'Beautiful Flyaway'

Michael: 'Beautiful Flyaway' was another 'ditty' ballad. I mean the other guys were on it, but it wasn't one of the big heavy songs'. Dennis: 'I love that song, especially the part where it speeds up; it reminds me of little Mozart. It's very Beatley, but that was Michael'.

It's an emotional ballad, unusual for the band to pull out a track that tugs at the heartstrings. It was written solely by Michael, who plays piano and sings lead vocals. There is sensitive accompaniment from the band, but this is mostly his show and it finishes with that nice sped up piano solo. It's the last bit of peace before the full-on assault following next.

'Lay Down And Die, Goodbye'

The spirit of *Pretties For You* returns. It's sequenced at the end of the album as a grand-standing finish, but it's not something that would appeal to everyone, being a listening challenge compared to the rest of *Easy Action*. Some people who might have heard it were The Osmonds. The blasting riff that Glen rips out at 1:20 is very similar to 'Crazy Horses'. It's possibly a coincidence but The Osmonds also 'paid homage' to Led Zeppelin's 'Immigrant Song' on 'Hold Me Tight' on the same album as their monster hit.

The track opens with the voice of Tom Smothers, from *The Smothers Brothers Comedy Hour* television programme, who says the apt lines, 'You are the only censor. If you don't like what I say, you have a choice, you can turn me off'. From there we are straight into a jammed workout with great fuzz playing from Glen before he hits the aforementioned riff. It's such a great riff you wonder why they didn't build a whole song around it.

The next section meanders a bit although Dennis gets in some interesting bass runs. Again it all breaks down, this time as a train approaches followed by what sounds like the dead trying to communicate from beyond the grave! At 5:35 a swirl of guitar/bass/drums starts to build faster and faster until at 6:50 we head into the outro. The surprise is that it's almost a song tagged onto the end of a jam. It's also familiar, being a slower, heavier version of the song The Nazz put out as a B-side.

The full band credits for this track don't include former member John Speer, who was credited on The Nazz single version.

Related Songs
'The Sound Of A' (Cooper/Dunaway)

Included here because it could have been on *Easy Action* if anyone had thought of it. Dennis:

> Alice, early on, learned basic chords on a guitar. Neal, to this day, still has this Spanish guitar with nylon strings that was always available sitting in the living room wherever the band lived. More of our songs were written on that guitar than any other instrument. Alice wrote three songs right away; he wrote 'Laughing At Me', 'Shoe Salesman' and 'Sound Of A'. The last one he forgot and we did that recently. Alice and Bob Ezrin called me and said, 'Dennis, who wrote 'Sound Of A'?' Alice said, 'Dennis wrote it'. I said, 'Well, you wrote it before I wrote it'. He didn't remember the song at all. We didn't have any recordings of it, but the melody was still in my head, so I decided to fill in the parts that I didn't remember.

Thanks to Dennis the song was indeed resurrected and appeared on Alice's *Paranormal* album. It's very moody, with a western movie soundtrack feel. That is enhanced by some of the guitar chord sequences, which are similar to the 'James Bond Theme' slowed down. It's great to hear Dennis and Alice together again on a song that goes way back in their past!

1971: Daggers And Contacts And Bright Shiny Limos

February saw the band finishing off their new album, while preparations started on the stage show. The band's lighting and stage designer, Charlie Carnel, was charged with building an electric chair to be used during 'Black Juju'.

The new album, *Love It To Death* had a confused release, owing to issues with the cover and the change of label from Straight to Warners. The album, their first classic, emerged on 9 March on Straight. The band toured heavily to promote it with the set-list staying solidly as: 'Sun Arise', 'Caught In A Dream', 'I'm Eighteen', 'Is It My Body'/'Going To The Graveyard', 'Second Coming', 'Ballad Of Dwight Fry', 'Black Juju' and 'Return Of The Spiders'. One of the best recordings from the tour, at Detroit on 1 March, gives an excellent idea of what the tour was like. Rather than ending the set 'in the light' with 'Sun Arise', as on the album, they start off with it and things get progressively darker. In 2015 Alice told Mike Alexander of *Stuff* how the show opened:

The stage was completely dark and I had a hammer. You couldn't see anything. All you could hear was clink, clink, clink, clink as I hit the mike with the hammer. Sparks would fly and people would go, what is that? And then, the sound of the band would come in with this huge baaa-oong, I'd sing, 'Sun arise' and the lights would come on. We did a really cool version of it.

Dwight Fry's escape on-stage would result in the death of a sadistic nurse, usually Cindy Smith, who said:

I got nominated to do it by the band because I was there and I was reliable. I'm not a performer; I prefer to be working behind the scenes in production as opposed to being on the stage. I took the part very seriously; I had empathy for the character and was very sombre. However, if I wasn't able to go to a gig for some reason, another person would get recruited for the part. Also, if we were in a city where a friend was attending, I would always try and talk her into the part.

April saw the release of a new single, 'Caught In A Dream', to capitalise quickly on the success of 'I'm Eighteen'. For those wanting to see what the band were like at this time, the show on 4 July at The Sunshine Inn, Asbury Park, New Jersey was video-recorded in black and white and is available on the internet. On 19 April there was a mouth-watering bill at the Civic Center in Ottawa, where the band supported Black Sabbath, with Yes as the opening act!

A delay in August at Chicago's O'Hare airport gave time for a rethink on Alice's make-up. Out went the spider eyes and the new 'Killer clown' face was born. It was also around this time that Neal's boa constrictor snake, Kachina, started to appear in the act.

September saw the band enter the studios again with Bob Ezrin, the first fruits of the sessions being the release of 'Under My Wheels' on 28 April. Further building momentum, *Rolling Stone* teased that the new live show was to feature a working gallows, handily being built on the Warner Bros. film lot, keeping things nicely in-house.

In October they embarked on their first European tour. The set-list remained the same as for the American dates, with one addition. 'Halo Of Flies' was inserted directly after 'Is It My Body'. The obvious addition would have been 'Under My Wheels' as it was the new single and intended to be featured on three television shows during the tour. Why this was not added to the set is a mystery, but 'Halo Of Flies' would prove to be a highlight every night. Dennis: 'When Neal did his solo we would all surround his kit and play along with him. I would be playing the tom-tom and Glen would be playing something else. That was us not wanting to do what everybody else was doing.'

While gigging in Germany, they recorded an appearance in Bremen for the *Beat Club* TV show, performing 'Under My Wheels' and 'Ballad Of Dwight Fry', although the latter was not broadcast. The footage is stunning, particularly 'Dwight Fry'. Thankfully a full recording survives, including the band setting up before the song. Michael puts in a rare appearance on the organ and Neal takes the child's voice on the intro.

A near-disaster happened on 29 April in Amsterdam. At their hotel, Glen got his arm cut in a revolving door and had to have stitches. Unphased, he carried on with the tour schedule regardless. In Paris, they were supposed to play at the famous Olympia Theatre, but the management got cold feet and the last-minute alternative venue was the Pierre Cardin Theatre. This was a much smaller venue and the combination of more ticket holders than the venue's capacity, plus a celebrity guest list, made for volatile scenes. In an effort to get in, a group of fans stole the actor Omar Sharif's Rolls Royce and drove it through plate glass doors into the lobby. The mayhem continued inside with the band turning in a great performance. Three songs ('Is It My Body', 'Black Juju' and 'Dwight Fry') were filmed in colour and used as part of a feature on the band on the French TV show *Pop 2*. Job done, the band headed to England but the repercussions of the Rolls Royce incident followed them there.

They arrived in London on 3 November with the first date scheduled to be at Birmingham's Kinetic Circus (held at The Mayfair Suite) the following evening. It's rare to read accounts from staff at the venues on the band's tours, but the Birmingham promoter Peter Martin and two of the security team, Dave Fisher (aka Derringer) and Jake Hawkins, spoke to me about the band's first gig in the UK.

It got off to a bad start because the truck with the lighting and sound equipment had not made it. Dave Fisher: 'All the gear was kept in Paris. The story we got was that some guy who couldn't get into the concert drove his car up the steps of the auditorium and through the doors trying to get in. So they impounded Alice's gear because somebody had got to pay for it all'. With the band unable to play, a rock disco was held instead, generously paid for by the band. There were additional bonuses for the Kinetic Circus staff too. Dave: 'I was given a crate of lager by Alice. He gave alcohol to everyone in the organisation there on the night to make up for not being able to play'.

Fellow security member 'Klondike' Jake Hawkins found Alice to be a surprise:

He came up to me and said, 'Are you a magician?' (because I had hair twice as long as his). I said no, and he said, 'Why's your hair like that?' And I said, 'I'm a professional wrestler when I'm not doing this'. And he started talking about that and American wrestlers. One thing I noticed was that all the time we talked he never swore, I thought that was funny. I mean bands would usually come out with effings and blindings. The other thing I didn't see was any drugs. Normally with them bands, there was plenty going on.

The gig was rescheduled for the following evening; the only free day left for the Kinetic Circus during the band's stay in the country. The band headed back to London, where they were due to film their *Old Grey Whistle Test* appearance the following afternoon. Despite Alice battling flu symptoms, they gave explosive performances on the *Whistle Test* of 'Under My Wheels' and 'Is It My Body'. The complete footage of them performing these songs several times is online and highly recommended. It's especially great to see Glen taking the solo on 'Under My Wheels', as he doesn't play it on the album. The cut short sleeve on his right arm is evidence of his accident in Amsterdam.

Following the *Whistle Test* session, the band headed back to Birmingham, where their first stop was back to the Albany Hotel, which had held their booking over. Peter Martin couldn't be there on the night, but he recalls how he got the booking, and stipulations he made to the band the night before. 'I spoke to my friend Barry, an agent in London, and he said, 'Listen if you want you can have Alice Cooper in the Midlands'. Alice Cooper was quite cheap, £400'. Barry had one crucial piece of advice for Peter: 'Be sure they know they can't be doing the thing with the feathers'. The 'thing' came during 'Black Juju', when for the crazed ending the band would split a couple of feather pillows and use a CO_2 extinguisher to fire them all over the place.

Fully warned, Peter spoke to the band: 'Listen, fellas, the Kinetic Circus is a Mecca-owned establishment and the walls are decorated with red flock wallpaper. I know part of your act involves feather pillows; we can't be having that in here. They questioned it, so I said, look it's been arranged that you don't do that here because it's going to cost somebody an awful lot of money. Anyway, they said, 'yeah we won't do it'. Dennis smiled wryly when I told him Peter Martin's story: 'We were full of promises that didn't come through once we got on stage.'

Dave Fisher was sent shopping by the band. 'Whatever the band wanted, I had to get. They asked for five pillows of duck feathers, which I got from Rackhams, and three CO_2 fire extinguishers, and £1 notes which Alice teased the crowd with'. Mission accomplished, he went to the hotel to collect the band. 'Although the Albany was practically next door we still picked them up in a car. At the hotel, I was stood in the lift with the band and my initial thought was, 'Man I have never seen so much hair in my life!''

The show made a big impression on him because he was also a fan of the band. 'We did a lot of bands there, but I tell you they were the most jaw-dropping. The sound was phenomenal and they were so different. They did the electric chair, and he had Kachina, the snake, there as well – on the side of the stage in an Ali Baba basket. Robert Plant was in the audience that night too.'

The time came for the 'thing with the feathers', which they had promised not to do. Dave: 'The pillows were piled on the stage, and me and a couple of lads were at the front to stop the kids jumping on. They turned the fire extinguisher on to the feathers and I nearly died. I nearly choked to death; you couldn't breathe'. Neal: 'The feathers were like a storm with the wrath of God.'

Peter Martin was livid when he found out: 'It went all over that ballroom and stuck to the walls. The manager from Mecca, who was there on the spot, was not happy. In those days you had to pay half of the fee up front in advance, and the other half in cash on the night. What I did was withhold the cash in this case while we sorted out how much it was going to cost to get all the flock off the walls'. In fact, the whole of the £200 cash on the night payment was withheld to cover the refurb costs. Michael Bruce laughed when I recounted Peter's story to him and said they likely needed a refurbishment paying for!

For Dave Fisher, it had been utterly memorable: 'When they'd gone and it was all over, I was sitting on the edge of the stage, all of those feathers were still falling slowly from the ceiling!' He got the new album, his ticket and a tour poster fully signed. These are cherished possessions of his to this day.

The band left to take the train from New Street Station for London but ran into trouble. Dennis recalled to me (at the 2002 *SickCon* convention in Crewe) that the train broke down in the tunnel, with a live cable having fallen onto the track. The band had to walk back along the side of the track into the station, carefully avoiding touching both the rails and the train carriage.

The band appeared at The Rainbow in London on 7 November. A full recording of their show survives in fair quality and is a good record of this historic tour. Their appearance got a lot of media coverage, heightened that week by the airing of the *Whistle Test* show on 9 November. The only blip in the UK was that the planned recording of *Top Of The Pops* was cancelled, probably because 'Under My Wheels' was not making any impact on the charts.

The band departed back to America where rehearsals were scheduled for the tour to promote their new album, *Killer*. The band had the ideal place now to write and record and for down time, having collectively bought the Galesi Estate, a mansion in Greenwich, Connecticut. The sheer size of it meant it was perfect for the band and their friends. The Ballroom was particularly useful as it was where they rehearsed and honed the stage-show, set to be more spectacular than ever before.

Joining for the tour was Dave Libert as tour manager. Dave had had his own spell in the spotlight as lead singer with The Happenings, who hit number three on the American singles chart in 1967 with a cover of 'I Got Rhythm'. He soon became a vital part of the organisation, ironing out the day to day challenges and ensuring the daily routines ran like clockwork. He later also appeared as a backing vocalist on the band's albums.

Killer was released in November, and by the end of the month, the band were playing 'warm-up' shows in South Bend, Philadelphia and Saginaw. These saw the début of the gallows hanging routine and the clown eyes make-up. The first show 'proper' of the tour came on 1 December with two performances on the same day at the Academy Of Music in New York. In the audience that night were Blue Oyster Cult. It proved, says the Cult's Joe Bouchard, to be a turning point for their ambitions. Joe:

We had tickets for the late show. What I didn't know was there were three opening acts at both shows. So the late show didn't start until after midnight and Alice wouldn't be performing until four in the morning! But I was a young lad and had loads of energy. As we were going into the theatre, we saw one of our roadies coming out. He said, 'Wait until you see Alice Cooper. I won't tell you what he does, but it's scary as hell!' So I'm sitting in my seat, getting real nervous, and I have to sit through three opening acts! Finally, Alice comes on and I was blown away. Every aspect of the *Killer* show was super tight and everything sounded great. Of course, he had the scaffold and a very realistic hanging scene, but I was flabbergasted by how tight the show was – the sound, the songs, the lights, everything was perfect. We realised we had miles to go if we wanted to have a solid music career.

The set-list for the first half of the tour was: 'Intro', 'Be My Lover', 'You Drive Me Nervous', 'Yeah Yeah Yeah', 'I'm Eighteen', 'Halo Of Flies', 'Is It My Body'/'Going To The Graveyard', 'Dead Babies', 'Killer', 'Long Way To Go', 'Under My Wheels'. The same intro was later incorporated into 'Public Animal No. 9' when that appeared in the band's set-lists in 1972. A major addition would come into the set as the tour progressed, and we will come back to that later.

A final 'first' worth noting was the use of taped effects. This wasn't common practice then and it may be they were the first band to use them. The first two effects were the sound of the baby cry on 'Dead Babies', followed by a female choir heard backing Alice's moans at around four minutes or so into 'Killer'. There is a noticeable pause after the choir tape ends and is then replaced by the third tape which is a recording of the martial drumming/bass/organ build-up to the hanging itself, complete with the priest's words. This tape was used to allow the band to perform the hanging sequence and prepare for the encore. The final tape was the thunder and lightning storm, which follows the sequence. With the use of these enhancements, the band were way ahead of their time. The gallows execution was not a big surprise if you had heard the album, but it got the band a lot of media attention. It looked dangerous and it really was; the safety harness has failed Alice on at least two occasions he has worked this stunt.

The tour programme surprisingly included a single-sided flexi-disc attached to the back cover. This featured 'Nobody Likes Me', the magnificent left-over from their first album.

The edginess and danger of the show were fully played up at one memorable gig at the Hollywood Palladium in December. Ernie Cefalu had heard that the next Cooper album was to be called *School's Out*. Already a fan of the band's music he created a comp of an idea to show Shep and Joe. They invited him to meet up with them after the show. Ernie is still amazed at what transpired:

I was absolutely blown away. There was a heckler in the audience. First, Alice pays no attention, but the heckler keeps tormenting him. At a certain point, Alice points at the guy and calls him up on stage. So the guy goes up on the stage and they get in this fight. Meanwhile, the group are still playing, then Alice pulls out a knife and stabs the guy. The guy falls over; people are freaking out, the lights go out, then the lights come on. Alice is in the straitjacket and they are walking him up the steps to the judge who sentences him to death. Then he was on the scaffold, the drums roll, and people are watching with their mouths open. He drops and the lights go out, that's it. Lights come back on a few minutes later and there's nobody on stage. The crowd are crazy; they don't know if he has died. There was no encore, that was it. This was all set up by Shep. He had advertised the show as 'If you have a weak heart or any kind of medical condition, you shouldn't come to the show'. He also said there would be nurses and doctors on staff at the show.

Events like this, though good publicity, led to problems. While venues were initially keen to have the band and their high profile show, they didn't want any negative publicity by association, or trouble with the city fathers in their town. Booking agent Jonny Podell recalled that 'Next time it was impossible to get them into the same venues. But that was my job to sort it out'.

The show on 17 December at the Saint Louis Arena in Missouri exists as a superb soundboard recording and was featured in the *Old School* box-set. The band are on fire and it's worth noting that there had hardly been a break since the end of the previous tour, and the bulk of the set was new.

By New Year's Eve, the set had subtly changed. At Toronto, during 'Long Way To Go', the band dropped in a new instrumental, which saw them jamming around the riff of 'School's Out', before a long wailing solo from Glen. Michael: 'There's nothing like playing live, you try an idea and see how it goes over. It was a good proofing ground for some of the stuff, like in the long jam when we started playing 'School's Out''.

Two marvellous albums released in one calendar year and yet the biggest years of their career were still to come.

Love It To Death (Straight/Warner Bros.)

Personnel:
Alice Cooper: lead vocals, harmonica
Glen Buxton: lead guitar
Michael Bruce: guitar, keyboards, backing vocals
Dennis Dunaway: bass, backing vocals
Neal Smith: percussion, backing vocals
with:
Bob Ezrin: keyboards on 'Caught In A Dream', 'Long Way To Go', 'Hallowed Be My Name', 'Second Coming' and 'Ballad Of Dwight Fry'
Monica Lauer: child's voice on 'Ballad Of Dwight Fry'
Produced at RCA Mid-American Recording Center, Chicago, November – December 1970 by Bob Ezrin and Jack Richardson
USA release date: 9 March 1971. UK release date: June 1971
Highest chart places: USA: 35, UK: 28 (in 1972)
Running time: 36:58

Originally released as their third album for Straight Records. It sees the start of the partnership with Bob Ezrin, who edited, refined and polished their songs. The intent was to give you the feel of a live show on vinyl and the sequencing makes it run like an unfolding set-list. Dennis explains the thinking:

> Some songs were written thinking this is going to be an opening song, or this is going to be a closing song. We would go in the studio with

Ezrin. Everyone would have written down what they thought the order should be. We would listen to each guy's order, then we would whittle it down and we would all decide what the song order should be. We always wanted to start with the rocker, live shows too, do a few rockers, start off strong and then shift gears and get more artistic. Build it up enough on side one to make you want to turn it over and play side two. Then we would hit them with rockers again, and then a big shift into more dramatic stuff and a bigger ending than on side one. That was what we always shot for.

The difference between the album and its predecessors is so great that this is effectively a new début album, setting a template for the following records. The segues used on the end of side two, which create a sense of flow, would be a trick they would also use on *Killer, School's Out* and the unedited quad mix of *Billion Dollar Babies.* 'Neal: 'When Bob and Michael started suggesting these ideas in these songs, and the segues, I knew this was something that had not really been done before of that magnitude.'

It's the album where the Bruce/Buxton guitar partnership clicks fully into gear. In 2018 Alice told *Guitar World* that: 'Glen was very futuristic, and when he was on, he was as good as anybody. Michael Bruce, on the other hand, was a great rhythm and riff player. He laid the foundation, while Glen went into outer space'. Michael concurs: 'My job was to hold down the rhythm, to create something everyone could play along to. I was the guy who held down the fort.'

The album cover helps cement the new direction. The dramatic black and white theme features two contrasting images of the band on the front and back. The 'black' front cover sees the band caught in a spotlight, pouting and posing, and there's a definite sense that this is not going to be a conventional record. The back cover 'white' photograph is a less challenging, more approachable look. The two images are part of what was originally planned for the album – a dark side and a light side, black and white. In the end, the album was sequenced as if it were the stage show, building to a climax. Queen subsequently used the black and white portraits and song sequencing concept for *Queen 2.*

Open the gatefold sleeve and there is the close-up of Alice's made-up eyes, staring right at you hypnotically. But it was the front cover shot that caused controversy as it had Alice poking his thumb out of his cape, just around crotch level. The trouble was it didn't look like his thumb! Some airbrushing, cover alterations etc. were used for assorted issues of the album, but the latest batch of reissues have all seen a return to the 'thumb' cover.

Dennis points out that the key to the quality of their output was, 'Thanks to Joe and Shep who had negotiated in our contract for artistic control of our album covers, the song order and everything. That's why our album covers were so good'.

'Caught In A Dream' (Bruce)

Neal: ''Caught In A Dream' was always my choice for the hit song off the album. I like it better as a song than 'I'm Eighteen'. But 'I'm Eighteen' obviously more people related to. It became an anthem and I understood the popularity of it'.

Dennis: 'The record company wanted 'I'm Eighteen' as track one and we wanted 'Caught In A Dream'. We did it pretty much how Michael wrote it.'

A great opening track, setting out immediately from the opening bars just how far the band have come since *Easy Action*. Michael plays the opening riff and lead guitar, with Glen taking the raunchy rhythm parts. Bob Ezrin plays an organ part that adds well to the grinding groove that keeps coming at you, while Alice delivers a perfectly measured vocal performance around the middle of his range. The developing confidence in the band is evident in lyrics like 'I need everything the world owes me, I tell that to myself and I agree'. It's startling to hear the band so effective and powerful as this after their first two albums.

It was released as a single in America (backed with 'Hallowed Be My Name') but only reached number 94. The single mix features a vibrant piano part by Ezrin which adds a different flavour. It can be found on the *Life And Crimes* box-set.

'I'm Eighteen' (Bruce/Cooper/Dunaway/Smith/Buxton)

The band's first absolute classic, and their first big hit. It was also the beginning of a beautiful partnership in the studio. Bob Ezrin told *New Musical Express* in 1973, 'The first thing we ever did was 'Eighteen'. Their original arrangement was eight minutes long and had a lot of excess bullshit. My job was first to transform stage arrangements into record arrangements, which was something they'd never bothered to consider. Ultimately it was a great rush to hear the two minutes 38 seconds version. I knew it would be a hit from then on.'

The song is built on a killer riff and a sparse arrangement that relies on the dynamic delivery for effect. Alice's delivery is spot on; the twist in the lyrics where he lists his woes but then his voice rises because he realises that in spite of everything, 'I'm eighteen and I LIKE it' is terrific.

Glen and Michael interweave their guitars well on the choruses and it's clever the way Glen's lead guitar licks pop right out at you, such as at 1:09. On the verses, there are two acoustic guitars filling out the sound, with one played through a rotating Leslie cabinet. That's the lyrical melody that sounds like an electric guitar you hear on every verse.

Alice's harmonica part is a legacy from the song's longer blues version, but, in keeping with the new direction for the song, is sharper and more succinct. The final notes of the song feature an organ which adds to the big finish but amusingly is the only time it appears on the track!

On stage, the song got expanded a little, and live versions up until 1974 would feature Alice riffing on lyrics from 'American Pie.'

Famously John Lydon auditioned for The Sex Pistols by miming to this in Malcolm McLaren's shop. It continues to remain a relevant outpouring of youth angst to this day. It is also the song Alice (band and solo) have performed most in concert.

'Long Way To Go' (Bruce)
This full-on driving rocker ends the one-two-three opening punch of the album. Some terrific riffing from Michael keeps it going while Dennis plays delightful bubbling bass runs and Neal powers it along. Glen's guitar solo at 1:46 stretches out beautifully over some tasty percussion work from Neal. His diverse use of percussion always meant the band had more going on in the rhythm tracks than other bands of their ilk.

It's a fairly simple track musically, although they still find space for a breakdown section with Ezrin back on piano again. One part that was not so simple was the vocals. Dennis smiles at the memory: 'It was a marathon of vocal overdubs. Michael and Alice sang those parts over and over until I never wanted to hear the song again'.

It features the title of the album in the lyrics but otherwise is a song that is slightly overlooked on the album. It never made the cut for the *Love It To Death* tour set-list but did appear for the *School's Out* tour.

'Black Juju' (Dunaway)
Cindy: 'My all-time favourite. The percussion parts are amazing! Neal and Den would get so locked into the groove; it was spellbinding! It shows how great they played together, right on the same page, so strong. Neal is still Dennis's favourite drummer to play with.'

Of all the songs on the album, this is the most reminiscent of the first two albums. For inspiration, Dennis soaked up the different atmospheres in the two rooms he composed the song:

We stayed at this old hotel in Buffalo and it had a utility room with a water heater. So I decided I'm going to write a song. I had this tiny guitar amp, but I plugged the bass into it and cranked it up, so it was really distorted, threatening to blow the speaker. I took the door off the water heater so you could see the flame in there and I'm imagining that it's this inferno. I thought OK, let me capture that mood. I kept playing that riff over and over because I thought I can't forget this till Glen gets back because I want him to help me with this riff. Finally, he came back and I said, 'Get your guitar. I want to show you this riff'. So we had the main riff that was under the chorus, and the feel of the verse on which Glen has these great kind of jazzy chords. Anyway, I thought I'm not going to try and write the lyrics right now. I want to wait till I can be in a situation where I can capture that mood again – an Edgar Allan Poe mentality. A week or two later we were at a club in Cincinnati where Ronnie Volz worked and we didn't have a place to stay. Ronnie knew this guy who was a frat at a fraternity house at a college campus that was out for the summer. He said there was nobody there so we could stay. I went up in this attic and there were some windows that hadn't been cleaned for years. With the sunlight coming in they looked kinda orange and you could see dust in the air in the rays of sunlight. Because that was so bright, the rest of the room was dark, and there was a mysterious kind of feel. It was really hot, but I thought, I'm gonna get my bass and a notebook and pencil. So I wrote the lyrics there.

This truly unnerving track was recorded live in the studio, with some overdubs added later. Neal added another two drum parts and the track probably remains the ultimate testament to his inventiveness as a percussionist. Neal: 'I'm very proud of my drumming on 'Black Juju'. It took a long time for us to get it right, but that song kicked some serious ass!' It's his hypnotic ominous rolling drum rhythms that enter first, a powerful sound echoing off the studio walls with the insistent bongo track adding more menace. Neal: 'You listen to the beginning and you hear the bongos in the back. For what I played (on that intro) it would almost take three drummers to do what I did. I played the most powerful parts live on stage. On all my kits, I have the real high-end bongo drums'.

Michael's organ then enters the mix. If it sounds familiar, it's because it was influenced by Pink Floyd's 'Set The Controls For The Heart Of The Sun', the band being a favourite of the Coopers.

Hushed muted guitar punctuates and we rise up to the main riff at 1:55. A change of dynamics at 2:25 releases the growing pressure, dropping down (literally) as Alice sets the scene.

At 3:45 the tempo changes again for the eeriest part of the track. Dennis's bass and the organ carry the melody into the hypnosis sequence, Neal tapping his sticks as a counter to the melody here. Alice is now whispering right in your ears as he entices us to rest. Just Neal's sticks and faint bass accompany as he invites us to, 'Sleep an easy sleep'. Neal's ticking percussion and eerie muted and high pitched sounds accompany Alice as his voice gains in authority. 'But come back in the morning', he asks as those rolling drums from the intro pound back in.

A soft guitar moans over muted plucked notes as we rise to the sudden shock of the wake-up cries. Back to the riff and a heads-down, full-on jam to the end of the song – a huge wall of noise over which, at 7:31, Glen unleashes a howling fuzzed solo that lasts for over a minute. Some high runs from Dennis over the last bars and it drops away to Alice's snatched breathy 'Black Juju'. A brief edgy musical coda concludes the paranoia.

'Is It My Body?' (Cooper/Dunaway/Bruce/Smith/Buxton)

It opens with a rolling, almost sensual, swing feel to it and those choppy rhythm parts that are a Michael Bruce trademark. Glen, for his part, plays a great solo at the 1:30 mark. You also can't miss Dennis, who plays a terrific counter-melody to the intro guitar riff. At 1:17 he gets off one of his trademark runs that we first heard back on 'Don't Blow Your Mind'. Neal peppers the song with cymbal strikes giving the percussion part added zip.

Lyrically it questions whether the prospective acquaintance does want to get to know them in more than a biblical sense! The frustrated tone in the lyrics isn't what you would expect to see in their song-writing at this stage.

The outro sees that ascending run from Dennis again, but rather than the expected big finish there's a slow winding down and fade out. On stage, they would include a great blues section, called 'Going To The Graveyard', which added a different dynamic to the song, and an equally tangential diversion to the lyrics. The band rehearsed the 'full version' for the album, but it was either cut down because of the length or because it was felt it lessened the punch of the track.

'Hallowed Be My Name' (Smith)

Neal: 'I have a huge ego, humbly speaking, about my ability. My belief in my talent, and Dennis's talent, Glens' talent, Michael and Alice's talent. So when I say 'Hallowed Be My Name' – that's the band speaking not me'.

In the studio chatter on the intro, you can just about hear engineer Brian Christian say, 'Don't count your carps before they're hatched'. Wise words, but not as wise as the lyrics to the song. The religious overtones look at the moral state of the people from the point of view of God. So it's a surprise this is solely credited to Neal when you would have expected Alice to have had a hand in writing it. It transpires that Neal too had a religious upbringing. Alice performs it like a prophet addressing his followers, linking it into the theme of the following two tracks.

The song drives along on Neal's percussion and a great organ/guitar riff that gives it a real urgency. A wild cry from Alice at 1:10 and some suitably edgy lead from Glen leads back into the verses. The song ends on an extended instrumental section, from 2:01, featuring some lively bongos from Neal, and snarly counterpoint guitar from Glen. A fill from Neal breaks it up and then everyone is back for the final chords.

Sadly it never made the live set, and this well-crafted, satisfying song deserves more attention.

'Second Coming' (Cooper)

A great, mature piece of song-writing which works well on its own, and as the set-up for 'Dwight Fry'. The second coming in question is that of Jesus. After some introspection – 'It would be nice to walk upon the water, to talk again to angels at my side' – he returns to earth at a time the world is in turmoil. Triumphantly he proclaims that, 'I just come back to show you all my words are golden, so have no gods before me, I'm alive'.

From here on to the end is a thrilling evocative instrumental led by Neal's insistent, almost martial, drums, and an achingly beautiful piano part played by Bob Ezrin. Gradually it fades away to just the piano, a few moments of peace before the shocking denouement.

'Ballad Of Dwight Fry' (Bruce/Cooper)

It turns out we have a man who is convinced he actually IS the second coming of Jesus Christ! There he is locked away as his 'lonely life unfolds'. The intro is genius, Ezrin's piano notes fading away as Michael's doubled acoustic guitars kick in with a slow hypnotic chord sequence. Michael: 'Bob was such a good piano player that I didn't mind writing it and letting him play it. It wasn't a big deal, but I look back now and wish I had played more'. It's unsettling right from the start, with the bass and drums melodically underpinning the tension.

The quavering child's voice is Monica Lauer. Neal: 'We knew her before we got involved with Joe and Shep. She would bring us food. She was in the studio while we were doing the recording. She did the 'mommy where's daddy' voice, I did it live in my squeakiest voice but nobody can do it like Monica!'

Alice outlines Dwight's situation. Tiredness and confusion are evident in his voice but he also modulates into a disturbing, sinister tone, notably when he sings about his daughter – 'I'd give her back all of her play-things, even the ones I stole'. It is one of the most memorable lines on any Cooper album. The agony as he gets increasingly desperate to escape, 'I gotta get out of here' was enhanced by Ezrin having him sing it in a strait-jacket while boxed in under a pile of chairs; method singing at its finest!

Ezrin recorded an Alka-seltzer tablet dropping into water and then slowed the sound down to get an explosive sound. That explosion heralds Dwight Fry's escape leading into an unnerving passage as he makes his way out. The 'insane' guitar solo by Glen is outstanding, tremolo arm and string bends that perfectly conjure up the mind of a man who is now way over the edge. Michael: 'Glen could hear something and play it in a minute. When it came to an original solo, he would go for a sound effect type thing which was neat'.

Once 'Dwight' is out, at 4:55, he sounds so naïve that you empathise with his predicament. But then it switches. That switch: 'I saw a man that was choking there, I guess he couldn't breathe' is a shock. Did he kill this man, or was it a heart attack? Whatever it was, he gets increasingly distraught and frantic – even more so when he is eventually 'captured'. Credit must go to the band for the spot-on musical backdrop to the closing section, in particular, which makes for an epic finale.

The song was a homage to Dwight Frye (with an e), who was an actor who specialised in supporting roles in horror films. He would be the deranged villain in the background, such as Dracula's Renfield. He died in 1943 but his son, Dwight David Frye, also acted and was a regular contributor to profiles that featured his father.

'Sun Arise' (Harry Butler/Rolf Harris)

The only studio recorded cover version by the group was a surprise to British audiences. What were the band thinking of by covering this hit record (no. 3 in October 1962) by that bloke who did fast painting and comedy on the TV? It was in fact one of the earliest 'world music' hits, with its roots in aboriginal beliefs, and was brought to the band by Alice and Dennis who loved it. The band's interpretation is a revelation.

The warmth and bounce of the intro is a surprise as it segues in from the frantic ending of 'Dwight Fry', coming in on Neal's percussion. It shouldn't work, but it does! Ending the album with this cheery, positive song offsets the growing darkness of the previous three tracks. The sun comes up and brings back life.

The rhythm of the song gives Neal and Dennis space to be innovative and they are clearly having a ball. The vocals are superbly put together. Michael's voice harmonises so well with Alice's on the choruses. The outro is a seemingly endless number of those choruses, with the addition of additional amazing backing vocals from the studio next door. Neal: 'There was a gospel group that was singing in the studio and there were some great singers. I wasn't in the studio when it happened but that woman singing, it's just amazing. I was asleep in the studio on the floor when the mixes were being done and I woke up and the headphones were lying about a foot away from me on the floor. I put them over my ears and I thought what the fuck this is amazing – those choruses going by at the end. I thought then that this was a hit album'. That glorious ending gets you every time.

Related Songs
'Fields Of Regret'

This song is featured on rehearsal tapes and was possibly considered for inclusion on the album. Given the issues with the recording of *Pretties For You,* it's no surprise that a song the band highly rated might get another chance to shine with Bob Ezrin at the controls. In the end, they passed on this, but there is one take in excellent quality in fan circles. It's three minutes longer than the version on *Pretties* – a notable difference being the inclusion of the end instrumental section from what was to be 'Killer' before the spoken word section.

'Going To The Graveyard' (Bruce/Buxton/Cooper/Dunaway/ Smith)

Usually listed on bootlegs as 'My Very Own,' but both Dennis and Michael confirm the correct title. Michael explains, 'That could have been a separate song on its own. That was the nice thing, we could take nice little bits there and extrapolate them into something or use them for a whole song.'

It is featured on live recordings from tours between 1970 and 1972 as the bluesy jamming interlude during 'Is It My Body?'. It's interesting to hear them play in this style, Dennis's prowling bass gives it brooding menace and there's nice guitar interplay as the track speeds up faster and faster before shifting back into 'Is It My Body?'. Strictly not a related song, but a related interlude!

'Bring Up The Light' (Dunaway)

Black Juju 'was Dennis's 'dark song' for the album. 'Then I wrote 'Bring Up The Light' which was going to be the light song'. It didn't make the final cut, but part of it has turned up since. 'The riff was complex and, like 'Juju', it required lots of floor toms. Michael must have had my cassette demo because he swiped the riff from me. When I heard 'When Hell Comes Home' (on the 2011 *Welcome 2 My Nightmare* album) I said, 'Michael that's my riff', and he just smiles!'

'You Drive Me Nervous'

The elements that make the song are there in three rehearsal takes. The psychotic nervous guitar part features and the basic melody is there. Principally missing is the phasing and the tight urgent feel. They knew they could do better and the song was shelved for the time being.

Killer (Warner Bros.)

Personnel:
Alice Cooper: lead vocals, harmonica
Glen Buxton: lead guitar
Michael Bruce: guitar, keyboards, backing vocals
Dennis Dunaway: bass, backing vocals
Neal Smith: percussion, backing vocals
with:
Rick Derringer: lead guitar on 'Under My Wheels', rhythm guitar on 'Yeah Yeah Yeah'
Bob Ezrin: keyboards, Moog synthesiser
Artie King: spoken words on 'You Drive Me Nervous'
Reggie Vincent: backing vocals
Produced at RCA Mid-American Recording Center, Chicago, 1971 by Bob Ezrin and Jack Richardson

USA release date: November 1971. UK release date: 5 February 1972
Highest chart places: USA: 21, UK: 27
Running time: 37:08

'*Killer* is the best rock album ever made, which, of course, followed the masterpiece *Love It To Death*'. (John Lydon in the notes for *Life And Crimes*)

The album is a gloriously thrilling cinematic experience, and the ambition and scale of what they achieve is off the charts. Everything is bigger than before with more impact, in no small part due to Bob Ezrin's fast-developing production skills. Another development is Alice's vocals. He was at his best on the last album, but he is even better on *Killer*, which sees him at the very top of his game, as indeed are the whole band.

The cover images are by Pete Turner, who was well known for his eye-popping wild-life colour photography, and many jazz album covers. His shots are the perfect vivid match for the music inside. The close-up cover image is Neal's snake Kachina, while the lettering was written by Dennis with his left hand (he is right-handed) so as to get the feeling that it could have been written by a serial killer. The back cover is one of the most iconic images of the group; it leaps out and grabs your attention. A differently tinted version appeared on the inside sleeve and several additional shots from the session were used for promotional purposes, including the *Killer* tour programme. The gatefold opens up to feature that infamous shot of a hanging Alice that upset parents everywhere. As if not provocative enough, it was a detachable calendar you could hang on your wall!

Among the guests, the album marks the first possible appearance by Glen's friend Rockin' Reggie Vincent (aka Vinson).

It's often cited as the best album by the original band. One who concurs is Dennis, who, despite still nurturing a love for the avant-garde *Pretties For You*, says, 'We were all playing at our best and we were all confident. The band was a complete unit, and it was still the band making all of the decisions'.

'**Under My Wheels**' (Bruce/Dunaway/Ezrin)
This is one of the greatest shots of adrenalin in the group's work. The core of the song was written by Dennis. He explained to *Goldmine* in 2019 that: 'When I wrote the song, Glen said, 'We can't make it a sappy love song'. I said, 'No, it's not, it's about a guy who has a brand-new

car and he's not that good at driving, but he gets all excited because he's going to go pick up this girl and take her to the movies. He's concentrating on driving when he goes over to pick her up and he doesn't realise she's already standing out on the kerb and he runs her over. It was just for the fun of it. I was thinking like Chuck Berry, you know?'

The verve and attack of the band firing full blast is evident from the opening notes. It comes crashing in, a huge statement of intent that the group mean business. There is a confident swagger in the music and the doubled rhythm guitar attack of Glen and Michael give the riffs real crunch. Great accents and fills from Neal too.

When it came to the solo Ezrin used the visiting Rick Derringer's take instead of Glen's. Dennis for one was puzzled by this: 'I loved what Glen played on 'Under My Wheels'. For some reason, Ezrin then buried Derringer in the mix behind a wall of unnecessary brass, instead of giving him the stage to let rip, as you can hear he was doing. Michael: 'I didn't even know that Rick Derringer had played that. It was already done and mixed. I was a little shocked, but he did the job. That was a song they did a thing called bus monitoring on to try and make the track a little more distorted and punchy. I remember the first mix we heard of it was just over the top. Bob went in and did another one because nobody cared for it; it was a little too saturated. The second mix was great.'

Alice's almost hiccuping cries of 'wheels' on the outro go right back to Buddy Holly. While Alice was channelling Buddy, was Bowie taking note of the Coopers? His later 'Suffragette City' sounds similar in parts. One who might agree is Michael who added the chorus of that song when he performed 'Under My Wheels' on his 2001 solo tour.

The song was released as a single (backed with 'Desperado') and got to number 59 in America and number 66 in Britain.

'Be My Lover' (Bruce)

Neal: 'A lot of the songs that became our most popular were written or started by Michael. Those melodies he has are very catchy. That's why he was brought into the Spiders because he wrote music'. Dennis: 'We put some pretty dramatic changes in it. It came in like that's the song, now all we had to do was write our parts'.

Two women feature in the song's lyrics. Kit Pandel was band publicist Ashley Pandel's sister and clearly made an impression – 'She struts into the room, well I don't know her, but with a magnifying glance I just sort of look her over'. The second was an elderly lady, sat on a plane next to

Michael, who wouldn't understand how the singer (a man) was called Alice! Michael: 'The first verse – she definitely caught my eye, she was a very beautiful woman. The second verse actually happened on the airplane. There was this elderly lady and when I said you really wouldn't understand, I thought it would go in one ear and out of the other. The first verse was back in the day in Detroit and on our way to making it big kind of mind-set. Verse two – now we're travelling around on the jet plane'.

It's a catchy, breezy song which drives along on a riff not dissimilar to The Velvet Underground's 'Sweet Jane'. Alice's conspiratorial vocals, with plenty of reverb, keep you hooked with the 'story'. Everything slows down and then builds into a burlesque section where Alice practically invites us upstairs. It's a suitably sassy ending, complete with Neal's twirled drumsticks dropping!

The song was released as a single (backed with 'You Drive Me Nervous') and got to number 49 in America.

'Halo Of Flies' (Cooper/Buxton/Bruce/Dunaway/Smith)

The band are at their pinnacle here for the most spellbinding track they ever recorded; it's a thrilling journey through their influences, with the twists and turns of a Hollywood blockbuster soundtrack. It consists of several sections of what were originally different pieces bolted together. It works because of the skilful linking, and it plays out exactly like a film score mirroring the changing scenes. The evocative title is a big plus, said to be a suggestion by Alice's then-girlfriend, Cindy Lang.

The first part opens with a pulsing guitar riff, doubled by Glen and Michael, sounding like a slowed down insistent siren. The only other sound is Neal's creative cymbal splashes, adding to the rising tension. At 0:25 the pressure drops and Dennis enters on bass for a short but melodic interlude before things step back up for a heavier sequence at 0:34. Ezrin's Moog blips are right out front here, but behind them, there is a clever riff played in unison by the rest of the band, with lovely drum fills by Neal at the end of each phrase. Change of pace again as a watery sounding keyboard comes in, and the music gallops (1:14) like a runaway horse.

The track is often singled out for Neal's drum parts. He feels that: 'The overall barometer for a drummer to play what I did in Alice Cooper songs is 'Halo Of Flies'. There's a swing beat to it like the classic big swing bands of the '40s. It's got that human feeling in there and that's the swing'.

At 1:33, the dense atmosphere clears as Alice enters. His phrasing is a constant delight, with the nod to 'My Favourite Things 'on the line' 'Daggers and contacts, and bright shiny limos' being one to savour. He runs through a gamut of spy movie tropes until the drama comes to a head at 3:28. If you had to distil the best elements of his voice down to a single word, then you can't top the goose-bumping power he gets behind the word 'flies' in, 'And I will smash, Halo of Fliiiiiieeeeeesssss'. As he stretches out the word, the band come back in hard and aggressive for a heavy riff sequence as Alice takes us overseas (as the James Bond films always do). With one final verse of spy references including the immortal, 'I put a time-bomb in your submarine', he realises in the end that, 'You never will understand'. With a tone of resignation, he leaves.

Now, at 4:33, we are off to the far east, for a sequence that sounds for all the world like something Wilson, Keppel & Betty would have done the sand dance to! At 5:10 Dennis's bass ripples up over some string effects from the Moog. The Moog dominates the melody until it drops down and away leaving an insistent throbbing bass line, soon joined by percussion. Way ahead of trends, what we get here now is a drum and bass solo.

Neal: 'We took the drums into the ladies' rest room of the RCA Studios in Chicago. Dennis gets that swing in the bass part he is playing under the drums and keeps it going. That gives me the open air to play the solo'. Dennis: 'There is an easier way to play that bass part, but I refuse to do it. We decided drum solos had become so cliché, so I said, we're not gonna do a drum solo we're gonna do a duo – a bass/drums duo. We all knew Neal was going to absolutely kill it.' And he certainly does, they both do! It doesn't outstay its welcome and it works perfectly in the context of the track.

At 6:30 Michael, Glen and Bob Ezrin come back in for the final rush to the end. A full-on assault attack based around the main theme and increasing in tempo. Somehow Michael or Glen finds space to get a guitar break in at 7:17 without interrupting the flow, which builds and builds to the final frantic riffs and the swooping climactic keyboard/Moog splashes followed by a huge musical orgasm and full-stop from the band. The end of a breathtakingly inventive track that proves beyond doubt that this band could seriously play.

It still thrills Cindy: ' I love to hear Neal and Den play 'Halo Of Flies'. Another awesome percussion piece. They lock right in and make it so powerful.'

The track was released as a single in Holland and Belgium in 1973, backed with 'Under My Wheels'. It got to number five in the Dutch charts and fifteen in Belgium.

'Desperado' (Cooper/Bruce)

Despite the writing credits, the song started off as Dennis's work. 'I wrote a song called 'Desert Night Storm' and I had the Spanish kind of feel, and then Michael changed some of the chords and Alice changed a lot of the lyrics. All of a sudden I didn't get any writer's credit. But I did get my name on some songs I had less to do with, so that was okay.'

Alice usually says it's dedicated to Jim Morrison, and that is conceivable given that the Doors' singer had died not long before they started recording, and he was a personal friend. Alice also uses his best Morrison-esque voice on the verses. However, he also has said that it was inspired by Robert Vaughn's character, Lee, in *The Magnificent Seven,* and this is credible given that the lyrics are a fair description of him.

The verses are suitably downbeat and sombre in tone, which makes for a contrast to the choruses which put the energy into the song. The acoustic guitar melody is one of the band's most attractive, while Ezrin adds Moog synthesiser strings to the mix that pick up on the reflective feel and contribute to the Western movie overtones.

'You Drive Me Nervous' (Cooper/Bruce/ Ezrin)

Dennis: 'It had been kicking around for years. We would bring the song up and there was always something wrong with it. When we were in the studio for *Killer* it came back off the shelf again. We loved the song, but it wasn't moving like it should. Ezrin said, "Neal play a straight beat, forget all that stuff", and that did it. All of a sudden, it took off.' Neal: 'It's flams all through the song, which is a basic rudiment of percussion'.

It's a scorching opener for side two. The band don't get anywhere near enough credit for their ability to rock out, and this is one of their best in that vein. A breathless ride powered along on Neal's drums and a rhythm guitar part to die for from Michael. Those 'nervous' guitar fills from Glen add the icing on the cake. Michael: 'That thing Glen did in the middle, you know, that wild whammy bar thing? Glen was ahead of his time with that. I was listening back after talking to you and all the little riffs I added in there add a lot to the flavour'.

Alice is superb, especially when he sings: 'You run around with all that hair, they just don't like those rags you wear'. The emphasis he puts on 'hair' and 'wear', stretching the words out, showing a vocalist oozing in confidence.

There is a sly nod in the song to Eddie Cochran, another disaffected youth. Alice sings 'Your mom and papa come up and said', to which sound man Artie King responds: 'Honey, where did we fail?', channelling the dialogue with Eddie's boss in 'Summertime Blues'. Everyone grinds out the final riffs which die away as Glen's guitar wails off into the distance. It's a simply stunning track!

'Yeah Yeah Yeah' (Cooper/Bruce)

Sequenced to provide warmth and light relief between the frantic assault of 'You Drive Me Nervous 'and the sombre 'Dead Babies. 'It's a deceptively low key track, missing much of the drama and dynamics of the rest of the album, but there's a lot to enjoy here. The change in tempo at 1:44 with a shrieking lead riff from Michael also features Alice on harmonica. You don't hear him play it that often, and here he gets in a harmonica solo. On top of that, he also delivers the classic pay-off line of, 'This is Alice speaking – suffer!'

Rick Derringer appears again, this time playing rhythm guitar, while Michael is on lead.

'Dead Babies' (Cooper/Buxton/Bruce/Dunaway/Smith)

An often misconstrued song. It is actually about the consequences of child neglect, but that message was easy to forget, or miss altogether, given that live versions featured Alice taking an axe to baby dolls! Dennis: 'It was put together from two songs, one had a great chorus and a lousy verse and the other song had the opposite. So I said, 'Let's take the good verse out of that song and take the good chorus out of that song and put them together'. I wrote a new bass line to tie the two together'.

Dennis opens the song with a slow heavily picked bass riff, the perfect intro for one of the grimmest songs in their catalogue. Michael and Glen join in with guitar arpeggios before Alice sets the scene with the 'killer' opening line, 'Little Betty ate a pound of aspirin, she got them from the shelf upon the wall.'

Betty's last call for mommy at 0.59 is almost unbearable, but it gives way to a chorus that is almost euphoric if you don't listen to the words! The family background is explored in the verses, but it becomes all about that chorus that gets right inside your head.

At 2.54, the mood and tempo shifts as a powerful, descending riff kicks in. Dennis and Neal join in adding to the intensity before Alice comes in with 'So long little Betty' etc. Another gear change at 4.04 builds up to the climax beginning at 4.33. It's an epic last minute or so with everything cranked up, the emotion pouring out as we hit more choruses. The brilliance here is the addition of a swelling brass arrangement (on the Moog). It all breaks down into an angry courtroom as the judge calls for order. A killer needs to be sentenced.

'Killer' (Bruce/Dunaway)

An insistent bass run cuts through the crowd noise with oncoming shards of razor-sharp guitars, flashing to the killer in the condemned cell reflecting on what got him to this point, 'What did I do to deserve such a fate.'

The instrumental break at 2:05 chugs away but could have done with being more dramatic. Just before the three-minute mark, things start to slow down to a stop. The 'wailing' and pained guitar sounds section that comes in at 3:35 could easily be used for headache medication commercials! Almost subliminally in the background, Alice recites the first verse again.

A brief pause and Neal starts up a martial drum roll, with Dennis's counter bass melody and some sad organ phrases from Ezrin. Listen carefully here too for the distant choir vocals. The priest (voiced by Alice) issues a blessing in Latin, as the killer is led to the scaffold. A few more power chords on the guitar, a pregnant pause and then the awful sound of the trapdoor springing. The Moog synthesiser ending that follows is an ear-splitting swarm of bees crescendo, a literal rush of blood, silenced sharply to nothing.

Archive releases
Detroit Rooster Tail 1971 (CD)

Recorded on 1 March at the Rooster Tail in Detroit on the *Love It To Death* tour. The CD running order has 'Sun Arise' in the middle and not as the opener, which is unlikely. Other than that, it's almost the complete set from the gig in very good/excellent quality, just missing the encore of 'Return Of The Spiders'. It's a highly recommended listen to hear the band as they were on-stage in that era.

Killer In St. Louis, 1971 (CD and Vinyl)

This soundboard recording of the band at the St. Louis Arena, Missouri on 17 December was officially released as part of the *Old School* box set. The CD includes the encore of 'Under My Wheels', while the vinyl just has the main set. The band are on great form for a well-drilled set made up of material from their latest two albums. The great version here of 'Halo Of Flies' proves they could play it live, with the drum/bass solo taking on extra impetus. Dennis: 'Even when I was in really top form, Neal would be blowing kisses and I would be like, hurry up, man I'm dying here!'

1972: Here Come The Jets like A Bat Out Of Hell

The *Killer* tour continued with scarcely a break for the holiday season. The 13 January show at Centre Sportif, Universite de Montréal was partly video recorded and presents a fascinating look at the bulk of the show. It was included in the *Super Duper Alice Cooper* set, making that indispensable.

Later in the month, on 30 January, the band played at Alexandria, Virginia. They were supported by Mitch Ryder who was touring with his band Detroit, promoting their debut album. On that album, and in his band, were future Cooper troopers Steve Hunter and Johnny 'Bee' Badanjek.

The new single, 'Be My Lover', was released on 21 February. The following month was supposed to see a return to the UK for two shows (on 17 and 18 March) at The Rainbow Theatre again in London. Although tickets went on sale, the gigs were cancelled due to The Rainbow going into liquidation. March also saw Richard Avedon take the famous pictures of a nude Alice with the new snake, Yvonne. One of these images was soon to bring London to a standstill.

A sign of the band's growing stature was their appearance at Puerto Rico's First International Pop Festival, running from 1 to 3 April. Also playing were The Allman Brothers, Faces, Emerson, Lake & Palmer, Fleetwood Mac and Black Sabbath amongst others. The Cooper Group played early on 3 April and their set was eventually released by Applebush Records.

By the middle of April 'School's Out', now with vocals, was in the set as a separate song after 'Long Way To Go'. It ran for around nine minutes, a looser version than the soon-arriving single, with a jammed section still as part of the song. Another minor set change was moving 'Is It My Body' from the middle of the set to after 'School's Out'. 'Under My Wheels' remained in place as a last rush of adrenalin for the encore.

Blue Oyster Cult popped up for some shows as the support act. For the Cult's Joe Bouchard, the pairing with Alice Cooper was a great fit. 'Our manager, Sandy Pearlman, said he only wanted us to play with groups that were "happening". Touring with Alice Cooper was that perfect situation. In 1972, as part of the *Killer* tour, we did twelve shows with Alice. We would have loved to do more.'

In between gigs the band had been rehearsing and recording material for their next album. The first fruits were the release of the 'School's Out' single on 16 May in America. While the single began its ascent up the charts, the band returned to the studio in June to record a topical follow-up – 'Elected'. The song would tie in with the American presidential elections, heading for the November vote.

A guest at the Galesi Estate and The Record Plant during recording sessions was Mick Mashbir, who was stopping off for a while en route to London. He was well acquainted with the band. Mick: 'In those days you could just show up at a friend's house and you would be welcomed. Mike Bruce and I already had a musical relationship from playing on his Wild Flowers sessions. Neal and I knew each other from our high school days, and Alice had hung out at my band house in Phoenix'. Mick was with the band for around two weeks and, without it being in any way pre-meditated, made a good impression at exactly the right time. Mick: 'They were recording School's Out and I spent time with them at the Record Plant. There was a room between their practice room and the kitchen. While the band was rehearsing, I was in that middle room playing along while Alice, unbeknownst to me, was in the kitchen, drinking beer, eating and listening to me'. Mick headed off to London, not expecting what was coming later in the year.

The School's Out album was released on 13 June in America and hit immediate trouble with part of the packaging. U.S. customs officers seized 500,000 pairs of the disposable panties intended to wrap the album, the said items falling foul of the Flammable Fabric Act. Alice was contacted for comment by an eager press and, never one to disappoint, he observed that, 'I know we're hot right now, but I never thought our panties would catch on fire'. That quote was lapped up by a delighted press far and wide, including Circus magazine. Warners defended their position on the underwear by stating that the panties were 'packing material' and shouldn't have to meet garment standards. The fuss blew over and the albums were subsequently shipped, complete with panties.

Late on in the tour, an explosive new finale to the show was trialled. For the 20 June date at Flint, Michigan there was a cannon instead of the gallows. Alice slid into the barrel of the cannon and waited in the space underneath. A climax of light and sound and then, with a bang, Alice (in fact a dummy of Alice) was to shoot over the audience into a net at the end of the auditorium. It didn't happen. Instead, the dummy got stuck, limply hanging out the end of the barrel. The misfiring cannon and dummy were taken off and Alice reappeared on the stage, as was supposed to happen, to sing 'School's Out'. Joining him was Mickey Dolenz, and they finished the set with 'The Monkees Theme'. They tried the under-performing cannon again the following night in Holland, Michigan but with similar results. Back to the gallows for Alice.

The last night of the tour was a one-off in London at the Empire Pool Wembley on 30 June. The arrival of the band in Britain and the release of THAT single was perfect timing. Glam Rock had reached its zenith in Britain and the Coopers' image fitted perfectly, with singles that suited the genre. All of the singles since 'I'm Eighteen' should have done well in Britain, but there was no stopping the march of 'School's Out' to spend three glorious weeks at number one.

The band arrived in London on 27 June and the following day recorded their appearance on *Top Of The Pops*. At least two takes were recorded of their performance. The first one nearly made it as a perfect take, until a final hitch. Michael: 'There was a girl by Glen and me. We asked her if we could lift her up at the end. As we lifted her, her skirt rode up with the camera on us. The director shouted 'cut' and we had to do it again'. Neal doesn't recall that bit of controversy because, 'I was always in my own world, I was just trying to do my own performance. This was a very live band so trying to put us in a bottle and make us do that was hard. You have to put pads over the drums and get cymbals that are made of rubber. They look real and you hit them and they move, but the sound is like hitting a couch'. The second 'keeper' take was the performance that sold the whole Alice Cooper deal for the ten-year-old wide-eyed me and thousands more in Britain. While the band were based in London, they hooked up again with Mick Mashbir, who was running a stall in Kensington Market when not playing guitar.

One of the most infamous Cooper Group stories happened on 28 June. A flatbed truck, carrying an enormous billboard of that naked picture of Alice with Yvonne, suffered a break down in Piccadilly Circus at rush hour. At the hub of the confusion, which lasted two hours, there was one simple fact: there was nothing actually wrong with the truck. 'No matter what they say, do not move the truck', Shep recalled telling the driver in his autobiography *Supermensch*. The stunt did the job, getting TV and press coverage (all alerted by the band's press office to the incident) and shifting the last lot of tickets to sell out Wembley. The driver was arrested but was taken care of by Shep, who paid him so handsomely that the money saved him from losing his house. Later on, the band adjourned for a party at Chessington Zoo which was attended by the UK national and music press. It was allegedly a party the like of which had not been seen before by a disbelieving press corps.

On 30 June, Wembley was THE place to be in London. Roxy Music supported, their debut album having been out two weeks by then. Although the gig was billed as the last performance of the *Killer* show, the band tweaked the set and started off with the B-side of their new single, 'Gutter Cat Vs The Jets'. This neatly book-ended the show, as they finished with 'School's Out'.

From there it was back to America for rehearsals for the 'School's Out For Summer '72 Tour'. The set-list was: 'Intro'/'Public Animal #9', 'Caught In A Dream', 'Under My Wheels', 'Be My Lover', 'I'm Eighteen', 'Is It My Body'/'Going To The Graveyard', 'Halo Of Flies', 'Gutter Cat Vs The Jets'/'Street Fight', 'Killer', 'Long Way To Go', 'School's Out'. A first-half packed with singles, and a punk-before-its-time 'Public Animal #9' stripped of the jazz textures and sounding like a caged animal breaking lose. The second half was dominated by the longer pieces before the final one-two punch. Tapes were used again for the same parts in 'Killer', while 'Street Fight' also used tapes to allow for the stage prep needed for 'Killer'. Theatrically the band worked up a gang fight for the 'Gutter Cat'/'Street Fight' section, leading into the gallows hanging which had been retained.

The first night of the tour was at the Henry Levitt Arena in Wichita on 12 July. In the audience was psychologist Dr Leslie Ruthven, who was taken along by the local newspaper to 'analyse' the crowd's reaction to the show. Showing real insight Ruthven observed that Alice's actions were designed to bring fear, shock, anger and emotional arousal. The audience, he said, were attracted to the stimulation and some would even get a feeling of relief when the concert was over. Maybe, but those interviewed by the newspaper said they were mostly there for the music.

One of the biggest gigs the band ever played came at The Hollywood Bowl, Los Angeles on 23 July. It remains a legendary performance in the band's career, a celebration of how far they had come on the road to success. The performance of 'School's Out' from this show was used as a promo video (synched to the audio from the single). It all finished off with a huge fireworks display and helicopters dropping those panties onto the crowd. The show came out as a bootleg vinyl album called 'You're All Crazier Than I Am' and even without the visuals it's an electrifying performance.

'Elected' was released on 19 September, and acted as an early preview for the next album. Back on the touring schedule, their gig at Hofstra University in Hempstead, California was partly filmed for the ABC In

Concert TV show. Because the show was nationally shown, it was the first real glimpse that most of America would have had of the band live. It produced a shocked response from the affronted and angry protests from those who lived in places where the transmission was pulled.

To Mick Mashbir receiving a telegram meant bad news, but the one he got on 20 September from Shep Gordon merely asked him to urgently contact the band's office. A few days later on a plane to New York, he wondered why they wanted him to play on the new album and what was up with Glen? He got there to find personal difficulties were going on. Mick: 'Mike Bruce suggested me. I assume, since they all knew me, they agreed with him and that was the beginning of my eighteen-month musical relationship with the Alice Cooper Group'.

The band and Mick got down to rehearsing the new songs, and on 8 October Bob Ezrin and the mobile recording studio arrived and they got down to trying to get some takes. Among things they did get down were the bed tracks for 'Slick Black Limousine', but things were not going well. Mick: 'By the 19th things were going so poorly that Bob Erzin wanted to pull the plug, but it was decided to press on once the band got to London. We arrived in London (4 November) and started recording at Morgan Studios the next day'. The studios were booked for a week to record tracks and vocals.

Following the week at Morgan Studios was the band's second European tour. The set-list was changed to accommodate 'Elected', which replaced 'Long Way To Go'. The first night, at Green's Playhouse in Glasgow on 10 November, was the only British date, as a proposed return to Wembley was cancelled. Alice told *Disc's* Caroline Boucher in November 1972 that, 'We've already done this act in London, and don't intend to repeat ourselves. We were going to put out a Christmas single saying, 'Enjoy this Christmas because it might be your last', but we decided against it'. The reaction to the show in Glasgow was incredible. Three rows of seats were wrecked, and some of the audience were dancing on the balcony ledge and throwing cigarettes down into the stalls. The ecstatic audience joined in word perfectly with the songs. Boucher observed that 'Going to shows mainly round the London area you tend to forget what audiences are really like, ones who enjoy themselves and leap about and get off on the band'.

From Glasgow, it was on to Paris for two shows in one night at L'Olympia. Seven songs from the first show were broadcast by Radio RTL, Luxembourg, while the second show was the central point of a film called the *Jukebox Special*. It captured the band arriving in Paris and six songs from the set itself. By the time the band reached Holland 'Elected' was moved to being the encore.

The German dates allowed for another appearance on *Beat Club* where the band recorded incendiary versions of 'Public Animal #9' and 'I'm Eighteen'. The first is an essential listen to a harder alternative version of the song. Michael: 'I always enjoyed doing that song live, the vocals and a lot of interaction'. The latter features an obviously drunk Alice somehow still giving it everything in a riveting version of the song. Neal feels strongly that, 'It's better than the single'.

They spent the early part of December in London and took in a special show on 9 December. Neal: 'We went to see The Who perform the orchestral version of *Tommy* with the London Philharmonic Orchestra. I had just bought my first Rolls Royce and I was chauffeur-driven to the performance, riding in my new Rolls for the first time. Some of the other band members came along with me. We were invited guests watching the performance. It was an amazing show! After the show, we were formally introduced and met The Who for the first time.'

On a grave note, Glen fell seriously ill at this time and was taken to hospital in London, where he was diagnosed with acute pancreatitis. He was released to fly home to Phoenix later in the month but immediately checked into Maryvale Hospital there. The problems for Glen had been coming to a head for some time. This latest development increased those pressures and was to have consequences for the rest of the band's existence.

School's Out (Warner Bros.)

Personnel:
Alice Cooper: lead vocals
Glen Buxton: lead guitar
Michael Bruce: guitar, backing vocals, piano on 'Blue Turk'
Dennis Dunaway: bass, backing vocals
Neal Smith: percussion, backing vocals
with:
Wayne Andre: trombone on 'Blue Turk'
Bob Ezrin: keyboards, Moog synthesizer
Reggie Vincent: backing vocals, guitar on 'Luney Tune', 'Public Animal #9' and 'Alma Mater'
Dick Wagner: lead guitar on 'My Stars'
Produced at The Record Plant, New York, 1972 by Bob Ezrin.

USA release date: 13 June 1972. UK release date: 22 July 1972
Highest chart places: USA: 2, UK: 4
Running time: 36:56

The band moved their operational base to New York for this album because, as Bob Ezrin told James Campion in his book *Shout It Out Loud*, it was part of the overall plan for the band to 'bust out' big. The Record Plant was selected for recording, with initial demos and run-throughs of the material done at the Galesi Estate. For Ezrin it would be his first time producing the band on his own; his boss Jack Richardson having been on hand for the two previous albums.

The album never seems to be chosen as a fan favourite, but one person who does pick it out is Glen Buxton. He told *Just Testing* that: 'The one I like best is really the *School's Out* album because I had a lot of freedom on it. I like jazz and all the chords, you know? The different chord changes in jazz'. Michael Bruce sees the album as an important stage in the band's development. '*Love It To Death* and *Killer* were like you guys are great, you got any more? But *Schools Out* was our break-through album. It really showed the depth of the writing'.

It's a more reflective record, not as immediate as *Killer*. There's only one single, which gives the impression of it being less accessible, but there is an enormous amount of riches to be found in the grooves in spite of that. The album had two big influences behind it, as Neal points out. 'The album is basically inspired by *West Side Story* and *Clockwork Orange*. Those were the two influences, image-wise and some of the music'. Another influence was the writer Gore Vidal, who is given special thanks in the album's credits. Alice name-checked him, and his 1969 book *Sex, Death And Money* in particular, as a key influence when talking to *Rolling Stone* magazine in March 1972. It was a book he returned to again for inspiration when he recorded a song of that title on his 2001 solo album *Dragontown*. Also given special thanks in the album credits is Chris Stone who was co-founder/owner of the Record Plant studios.

I contacted Reggie Vincent back in 1999, and he explained that 'I was the original session guitarist when GB was sick. They used me when he couldn't be there'. He is credited on the album sleeve, but the songs he played on (listed in the credits) are those he told me about.

The album packaging was astonishing – an opening school desk with legs. It was the first design that Ernie Cefalu put together for the band:

I showed them the desk, pulled the legs down and set it up, and lifted it up and pulled out the record. I had put one in there in a regular Warner Bros sleeve. Shep took the sleeve off the record and put the pair of paper panties on it. He said, 'Let's put the record inside these panties', so that was his idea. Right after that, I started working on it, but we left and started up Pacific Eye And Ear.

The details inside the desk were equally impressive. Each band member carved their names onto a real desk to be photographed! Inside it you found images of all the kinds of things you might find in a school desk and some you might not – crayons, marbles, a slingshot, and a switch-blade. Early copies of the album also carried a school report card with the track credits. Inside the desk lid is a picture of the band looking like it was taken in an alley, a pictorial reference to what you were going to hear. And then there were those disposable paper panties, optional in most school desks but we will give them some artistic licence there.

'School's Out' (Cooper/Bruce/Buxton/Dunaway/Smith)

The song that above all others in the back catalogue has gone on to become recognised, it seems, by almost everybody. The opening attack of that riff still rattles the speakers and stops you in your tracks to this day. It was a double-note lead that Glen had been playing for years, but, as Neal recalls, 'We never had the right place to put it, where it would work'. It was a riff that Dennis says was pure Glen, 'It was his personality, his attitude. It set the feel of the song'.

The lyrics capture the energy of the song too. The lines that make me smile every time are, 'Well we got no class, and we got no principles, and we got no innocence – We can't even think of a word that rhymes'. A classic pay-off at the end there, which came from Dennis.

The chorus has Alice right up front in your face with Neal's bolero drum beats, giving it a real sense of urgency. Dennis points out a simple but effective trick he uses on the chorus: 'Any bass player in the world besides me would play the low G with Neal doing that drum pattern. I'm sure Chuck (Garric) plays it that way, as well as everybody else who has played with Alice, but I found it to be muddying up the drums. You can't hear those floor toms as clearly, and that's why I play up the neck, an octave higher. We did a lot of things like that'.

Cindy enthuses about what the dynamic duo achieved: 'It's such a great anthem with such a pounding rhythm. The drums and bass are killer and pounding rhythmically right in the groove.'

Then there's the kids. Bob Ezrin's idea to add children's voices to the chorus, and their ecstatic cheers on the outro, make a real difference to the song's connection to the audience. He recruited some stage school kids from Central Casting who didn't quite know what to expect. Bob recalled their reactions to David Konow, of *Consequence of Sound*, in 2017: 'They walked into the hallway, saw this group and they were ready to turn around, get back in their taxis and go home! The kids were scared to death, but I got them all to relax, and we all had a really good time. By the end of it, the kids were all giggling and laughing, and they loved Alice.'

The origins of the title are often said by Alice to be from an old Bowery Boys movie, but there is an intriguing other connection. Alice has in the past expressed an interest in serial killers and even recorded an album about one (*Along Came A Spider*). On 26 June 1970, the Zodiac killer sent a letter to the *San Francisco Chronicle,* which was syndicated across America. In it he uses the phrase, 'school is out for the summer'. The phrase sounds common, but the only popular cultural reference to it came first in this letter. Alice, I feel sure, would have read that letter in the newspaper.

'School's Out' distils everything that is great about this band into one song. It was, of course, released as a single (backed with 'Gutter Cat'). 'It got to number seven in America and number one in Britain. Unusually for a single, it's actually longer than the album version due to the extended fade-out.

'Luney Tune' (Dunaway/Cooper)

This is a big change of mood after the jubilant title track. The 'formula' of two 'up' rockers to open the previous two albums doesn't happen this time. Alice goes from one 'prison' (school) to another. This time it's an asylum. Dennis, who Alice gleefully christened Doctor Dreary, is the main inspiration for this dark tune.

Lyrically it's the harder-edged flip to 'Dwight Fry', tougher and grittier. 'I'm swimmin' in blood like a rat on a sewer floor' is something you don't want to imagine. It's got some interesting things going on musically. Dennis and Neal carry the tune while Michael runs up and down the guitar harmonising perfectly. Glen's guitar fizzes on the edges of distortion and bursts over at 1:07 and again and again.

At 2:27 we head into a long instrumental outro with a beautifully scored string section over the top of the band. The jazz tones that crop up all over this album dominate the ending with Dennis's bass high in the mix as it slows to the crashing final chords.

'Gutter Cat Vs The Jets' (Buxton/Dunaway/Leonard Bernstein/Stephen Sondheim)

Dennis: 'I never really played chords; I only played a fifth, so I played two notes at the same time. I did that because chords have a tendency to overpower the speaker. It sounds muddy when you play a full chord. On 'Gutter Cat', basically, I'm just playing the two top strings'. This is an absorbing portrayal of a rumble between two rival gangs, scripted and scored almost as if it were a film; music and lyrics working in tandem to set and expand the scene.

The opening bass part is a scene-setting slow run along the frets and a lovely stretch at the end. Dennis: 'That was something I played and that they liked. So it was like why don't we have it fade in on that and then go into the song'. It perfectly conjures up some quiet back streets as they slowly come to life. Alice, as the Gutter Cat, sticks closely to feline analogies to describe his lifestyle, 'I met an alley cat, pussyfootin' around'. The interplay between the instruments is captivating, with Ezrin adding a great Moog synthesizer part to the mix.

Halfway through, the mood changes and at 2:23, we meet The Jets. The tension mounts in the music and Alice's voice drops to quiet menace. Adding to the growing tension, the *West Side Story* style finger clicks come in at 3:07. It would have been startling to hear them back in 1972 and it still has that effect now. There's real danger in the music and the swirling textures conjure up two gangs moving into position, circling around each other. The killer punch comes at 3:26 when the familiar musical motif from *West Side Story* comes in. Neal: 'Playing that part, oh man I couldn't have been more in heaven. We didn't do too many cover versions, but put Bernstein in there, count me in!' Michael adds: 'The jazz/juvenile delinquent thing fitted right in with school. Bob (Ezrin) thinks out of the box and contacted Leonard Bernstein, who gave us permission to do it. We worked it in just enough to not go overboard and it really helps on the album'.

In true Broadway fashion, The Jets get their verse in the spotlight now (at 3:52). The opening lines are those as quoted on 'Still No Air'. There's no backing down now and the music cascades into a final unison chord smash and 'pow' from the vocal choir.

'Street Fight' (Cooper/Bruce/Buxton/Dunaway/Smith)

This is a sound effects track, with some vocals, all underpinned by a
pulsing Dennis bass line and Neal's muscular drumming. Dennis: 'That
was a bass riff I spontaneously started playing as Neal and I were warming
up. Typical stuff for us but Ezrin recorded it and we used it.'

Dennis also says the sound effects were mostly down to Glen smashing
things up in the studio, Focus on the rhythm track and the whole thing
sounds far more interesting; otherwise, it outstays its welcome, even at 53
seconds.

'Blue Turk' (Bruce/Cooper)

The band's love of jazz finds its voice most emphatically on this track.
Michael: 'I'm playing piano on that. That guitar solo is what Glen was
naturally drawn to. We didn't do a whole lot of stuff like that'. It's also
a stand-out track for Glen too, who told *Just Testing* that: 'It was about
a jazz band at four in the morning playing a club where there's five
people there. We could relate to that from the early days. I had about a
four-minute freedom solo. I always liked that, and I had fun with it'. His
sister Janice recalls when Glen's love of jazz began. 'When we moved to
Arizona, my brother Ken stayed in Akron to finish his senior year. We took
his record player and records in the move. Because we knew we weren't
supposed to touch his stuff, Glen and I were all over it. Glen used to
listen to the Dave Brubeck album, with 'Blue Rondo A La Turk'. We both
liked it. That's where his love of jazz came from'. That explains the song's
title as a homage to the Dave Brubeck piece.

It kicks off with Dennis's mesmerising descending bass sequence.
Down the fretboard he goes, pauses, and off down again. There's also a
tremendous trombone solo courtesy of Wayne Andre, with Glen playing
his heart out in keeping those jazz licks going on and on. It suits Neal
too who shines on percussion, working around, and with, Dennis. Neal:
'When we play together we know where each of us is going and it is
amazing. He makes a change, then I make a change and it just flows
together. We are on the same wavelength when we are just jamming
freestyle'.

There's a confessional quality to the vocals, with Alice facing up to the
rigours of another show, 'I shiver, but I love this game'. The outro, as
Dennis goes down lower and lower and lower until you swear he will run
out of fretboard is deliciously hypnotic. It remains one of the best tracks
the band ever recorded.

'My Stars' (Cooper/Ezrin)

This is one of the most intense songs the band ever recorded.

Neal: 'It was one of the last songs we wrote on *School's Out,* and it was musically a segue to where we were next going with *Billion Dollar Babies'.* It was also the song that Dennis nearly missed out on, as Michael explains: 'Dennis was sick in the hospital so I played bass and Neal played drums and Glen was on guitar. We worked it up and when Dennis got back he goes, 'Would you want to play that on the album?' And I really wanted to say yes, but I said, 'No, Dennis, you're the bass player you need to play it.''

Dennis loved what he heard: 'I was in hospital in Toronto, so Michael actually wrote the bass part. When I got back, I was still supposed to be in hospital. We were due to go on the road and Shep wondered whether to get a replacement. I ended up doing part of that tour in a wheelchair because I wasn't recovered yet. They played me this song and I thought 'Oh man that's amazing', and Michael hands me the bass and says you can write your Dennis Dunaway part, whatever you want to do. I said I have some ideas for it, but I love what you wrote and that's what I'm gonna play. So it's pretty much Michael's bass parts.'

The song has a foreboding intro with howling guitars and an almost classical piano part of ascending arpeggios, which gives way to an insistent hard rock song full of twists and turns like a storm hitting. Ezrin's piano punctuates the mood with that intro melody and then joins in the rolling waves of sound coming at you. 'All I need's a holocaust to make my day complete' sings Alice and that's what we get. The jamming outro is superb, the band reaching new highs as everything builds up to a peak and then comes down to land. During the wall of noise, Alice throws in a repeated 'Klaatu barada nikto', the words used to stop the robot Gort in the film *The Day The Earth Stood Still.* Michael: 'He comes up with these things and I thought that was great'.

'My Stars' is also notable for the first appearance on a Cooper record by Dick Wagner. He plays the mind-blowing lead guitar fills and solos. Dick was next door in Studio A at the Record Plant recording the Ursa Major album with Bob Ezrin and pretty much the same engineering team. So in Studio B, when Bob decided they needed him for this song, he didn't have far to come! Dick states in his autobiography that he got $75 for the session and his name in the credits. 'Welcome to the big time', recalled Dick, but crucially it was the start of the Cooper/Ezrin/Wagner partnership.

'Public Animal #9' (Bruce/Cooper)

Back to the jazz feel again as Neal opens up with some terrific work on the snare drum. Dennis matches him all the way and Bob Ezrin throws in some jazz phrases on the piano. The backing vocals come in adding to the groove with those 'hey hey hey yeah' punctuations. Now Alice grabs things by the scruff of the neck with the opening lines, putting us right there in class. He almost snarls his picture of his world, 'Me and GB we ain't never gonna confess, we cheated at the Math test, we carved some dirty words on our desk'. GB being the ever rebellious Glen Buxton. The picture the lyrics continue to portray is real and recognisable, including his father: 'Old man waiting by the monkey bars, trading all his ball cards'.

The hot swinging rhythms, almost Motown in feel at times, and the wails of Glen's guitar give Alice the perfect backdrop. By the end of the song, he is reduced to an animal. Feral growls where words are no longer needed, before briefly breaking back into his top register. If they had have picked another single from the album, this would have been the strongest contender. It's a masterful piece of work.

The song was reworked for live dates, being much heavier and intense, losing the loose jazzy feel from the studio version.

'Alma Mater' (Smith)

This diverse album now pulls out a gentle, nostalgic paean to school days. Genre-wise this is close to being a country and western tune with a Roy Orbison feel on the guitars! It opens with a shower of rain, the returning use of Alka-seltzer dissolving and amplified – how's that for a subliminal message?

Alice is meant to be phoning this in, literally, from a phone box, hence the treated vocal effect. The anger and bitterness of 'Luney Tune' and 'Public Animal No. 9' are forgotten now. All that is left are the good memories of the best of times. The song connects with personal reflective lyrics which are funny, touching and sweet. You can relate to the experiences. The country feel, acoustic guitars and sensitive bass and percussion work are the perfect accompaniment.

Every time I see Alice live I long for him to pull out 'Alma Mater' (or the next decade's 'Former Lee Warmer') for the slow song, instead of 'Only Women Bleed'. That would be terrific. Neal did just that when he sat at the front of the stage and sang this with Bouchard Dunaway Smith on their 2002 British tour.

Tagged on to the end of the song is Dennis and Reggie Vincent, recorded in rehearsals, playing 'Happy Trails'. Reggie Vincent: 'They just left the tape running, and Alice said to leave it on the record'. The distant coyote calls, actually Dennis, add to the atmosphere. It all slowly cross-fades away to the 'closing credits'.

'Grande Finale' (Mack David/Bernstein/Ezrin/Cooper/Smith/ Dunaway/Buxton/Bruce)

Neal: 'It's still one of my favourite songs. It's got so much, from *West Side Story* too you know, and that's still one of my top ten most influential albums. I used to stand in front of the mirror and comb my hair back like a greaser, and I was in like fifth grade. Everyone in the band also loved the *(West Side Story)* album'. Michael: 'I heard the basic track first from Bob; it seemed to fit with the *West Side Story* thing. Bob was looking for something to finish off the album'.

This instrumental summing up of the album has no Alice on it, other than him joining in for the one word 'Pow' at the end. It's a funk-tinged jam, for all the world like the closing credits to a film. If your tastes stretch to this kind of workout, you are in for a real treat, because it's a wonderful piece of music, another example of the band showing off their considerable chops.

It's a relaxed jam for the first half, with Bob Ezrin's stunning brass and strings arrangement acting as a counterpoint to the band's hot grooves. There was a vogue later on of rock bands playing with orchestras, but I don't think anyone got as close to it working as smoothly as it does here.

At 2:24 Neal breaks it up with a terrific turn around on the kit that I spend all the song till that point waiting for. He just nails it. It's a release and we are off as the tempo picks up. The strings really come into their own in the second half here with the Moog fizzing underneath; it's a jaw-dropping arrangement – a huge panoramic sound. Glen delivers a magnificent wailing solo, what is in effect his studio goodbye to the band. The ending sees the return of the *West Side Story* vamp before that final 'pow!'

The songwriter credits are understandable, except for Mack David. He wasn't involved in writing the *West Side Story* excerpts; there are no lyrics here and he is a lyricist. Was this an error and the credit should have gone to Stephen Sondheim?

Related Songs
'Call It Evil' (Cooper/Bruce/Buxton/Dunaway/Smith/Reggie Vincent)
This sessions out-take first appeared officially on the *Old School* box set.

Co-writer Reggie Vincent was present and plays on it. It has a similar feel to 'Gutter Cat' and it shows promise. It could have been worked up and fitted in on the album, and maybe would have done if Ezrin hadn't pushed for 'Grande Finale'.

Archive releases
Mar Y Sol (CD and vinyl)
The band's set on 2 April 1972 at the Mar Y Sol festival was released by the Applebush label in 2017. The full set is featured apart from the encore of 'School's Out' which had been officially released already on the *Old School* box set.

The sound quality is excellent, if balanced a little too high in favour of Alice's vocals. At times it gets a little ragged. Alice, for example, loses his way in 'Yeah Yeah Yeah', but on the other hand they pull off a tight version of 'Halo Of Flies'. In the 1972 live versions, Alice would drop the line 'But I still did destroy her', as he does here, and replace it with 'But diamonds are forever', a reference to the Bond film that had come out in December 1971. Neal nails the drum solo, one of the best versions, while Dennis somehow keeps that pulse going. It's also great to hear 'I'm Eighteen' with the bluesy introduction they used on this tour for the song.

1973: Ready As This Audience That's Coming Here To Dream

Cash problems of a sort came at the start of the year with the Treasury Department. The band's photoshoot with David Bailey included the image of the band surrounded by piles of banknotes and the Treasury had a problem with it. The Secret Service had refused permission for Color Services of Los Angeles to print the packaging because of that image. A 1968 directive stated, 'It is not in the public interest to grant any special exemptions from the law which prohibits colour photographs of currency'. The Secret Service Counsel, however, ruled in the band's favour declaring that the currency as seen in the Bailey photograph was not of sufficient similitude or likeness to cause a problem.

The first single to promote the album was released on 16 January. 'Hello Hooray' was selected as the crucial trail-blazer. 'Elected' had already been released, but way before the new album was on the public's radar.

The band were enormously popular in Britain, so the band decided to say an unusual thank you. The *New Musical Express* got a great response when they gave away a flexi-disc of Mick Jagger introducing excerpts from 'Exile On Main Street', so the idea was rolled out again for 1972's hottest band. 'Slick Black Limousine' was given away with the 17 February issue of the *NME* backed with excerpts from the album.

February was originally planned to feature a run of dates at the Palace Theatre in New York – 'Alice At The Palace'. Ernie Cefalu got as far as designing a poster, but in the end, it didn't happen, either due to venue concerns about the nature of the act, or excessive ticket demand or union problems. A mix of all three reasons was likely behind the decision. In the end, the huge show they had planned for the dates became the tour they took round North America to promote *Billion Dollar Babies*. The public would get the chance to see the band's most spectacular production so far, initially set as 60 dates in 56 cities, a mammoth undertaking.

The band put the set together at the Galesi Estate. Glen was to play on the tour, but it was decided to augment the line-up with Mick Mashbir, who had done such a sterling job on the album. Also added was Bob Dolin on keyboards, which would mean the keyboard parts for the new tracks were better covered than with Michael juggling roles as on previous tours. Michael welcomed both men:

Mick had a great look and he was a savvy guitar player. Bob Dolin was a piano player, but he could do all the synthesiser stuff too. Keyboard players are one thing, but piano players are another. He had that depth to play the stuff Bob Ezrin was doing and I wrote. That's the reason we needed him.

Billion Dollar Babies was released on 25 February in America. The same day the band played a full dress rehearsal for the tour (with no audience) at Port Chester in New York. As well as working through the set-list, the stage performers also had to get used to the new stage set, designed by Joe Gannon. He had produced a huge impressive framed construction on two levels, like a giant Meccano set covered in chrome! Steps led from each level and there was a framed entrance below Neal's position. The entrance was dressed with pieces of mannequins and statues, but what drew your attention most, behind Neal, was an Egyptian sarcophagus. This would open out during the show and shoot out lasers during 'My Stars'. Adding to the impact were powerful white super trouper follow spotlights that lit the band (and especially Alice) in glaring contrast to the ambient lighting.

The giant set meant they had to play stadiums and arenas in America, but by now they were the hottest ticket in the country. The venues that wanted the show were prepared to do what it took to accommodate them. Jonny Podell: 'After all it's show business, and once they started selling tickets nobody cared at all about the increased production issues'. February ended with Alice posing for the Salvador Dali hologram project, which would be unveiled later in the year.

It was decided to open the tour in Canada, away from the glare of the American press while things were bedded in. The first night was on 1 March at the Kitchener Memorial Auditorium in Ontario. Mick Mashbir:

A couple of things stand out. The first gig, because I had never played for 10,000 people before, and the last show when I leaned over to say something to Mike Bruce, slipped and fell as the lights were coming up. I still have a scar on my ear as a memento. The time in between those moments is a blur of sex, drugs and rock 'n' roll.

The support band for the tour was Flo & Eddie, who were promoting their second album, *Flo & Eddie*. This was produced by Bob Ezrin, who also played piano on it. Guesting on guitars were Steve Hunter and Dick Wagner!

The band's formula for putting together a set-list reached its zenith on this tour. Neal: 'We knew how to build a set. We had three sections, the intro where we would do the real 'up' songs, then the dark songs, and then the finale. Again it was about the dynamics and the music in the songs that we chose'. The set-list was:- 'Hello Hooray', 'Billion Dollar Babies', 'Elected', 'I'm Eighteen', 'Raped And Freezin'', 'No More Mr. Nice Guy', 'My Stars', 'Unfinished Sweet', 'Sick Things', 'Dead Babies', 'I Love The Dead', 'School's Out', 'Under My Wheels'. 'They used a tape of Mussorgsky's classical piece 'Night On A Bare Mountain 'as two interludes, and a taped performance of 'God Bless America' after the encore. The only set change was an additional encore of The Beatles' 'Hard Day's Night' on the very last night. It was a fair summary in one song of the tour!

The new album was naturally heavily featured in the set-list, with only 'Mary Ann' missing. It wouldn't have worked in the stadiums, and they replaced the light relief it offered on the album with 'Dead Babies', which says it all! The shock was that inclusion of 'My Stars'. It wasn't featured on the previous tour as they had no dedicated keyboard player, and compounding the problem was that Dick Wagner had played the extensive solo too. Now, with Dolin and Mashbir in tow, it was possible and it proved a highlight of the set.

Also part of the act were Cindy Smith as the dancing tooth for 'Unfinished Sweet', and the magician The Amazing Randi (James Randi), whose job it was to extract Alice's decaying molars and also be hands-on with the guillotine. The deadly blade was the new cutting edge method of execution for Alice. The safety catches made it less risky than the gallows, but it apparently took Alice a while to get his nerves steady enough to try it out. The final member of the stage party was a President Nixon lookalike who came out as the band paid homage to the stars and stripes while Kate Smith's rendition of 'God Bless America' played over the P.A. 'Nixon' was unceremoniously given a rough welcome by the band and escorted off, only to return every night.

Mick Mashbir and Bob Dolin were not hidden on stage, but they were not given any focus as being 'part of the group'. Mick:

Bob and I were definitely treated as side men. We never took limos from the airport to the hotel. We rode on the crew bus. This was because the press was usually waiting at the hotel, and management didn't want them approaching us and asking questions. Through the whole tour, my name wasn't in a single article or review. One time Alice came over to me during my solo and the spotlight was on us both, so management put a stop to that as well. When I was soloing, they put the spotlight on Glen. I accepted that because I was playing in front of 10,000 people, and that wasn't too shabby. I understood that it was all about the band's image and Shep was the guardian of that.

The first American date came on 5 March at Rochester War Memorial in New York. The set-list was slightly different (and may have been on the previous shows too) with 'Hello Hooray' opening the show as a shorter intro arrangement, and then being played in full after 'No More Mr Nice Guy'. Dennis didn't remember the set change, but on hearing a recording of it commented that 'It sounds deliberate, all of the instruments stop simultaneously'. 'Hello Hooray' just sounds wrong though anywhere other than opening the show.

The dates followed thick and fast with the band and crew travelling on their own plane between gigs. This was the Starship, which Led Zeppelin also used and can be seen in their film *The Song Remains The Same*. There was an unexpectedly larger gap in the schedule after the Williamsburg show on 11 March when the date in Knoxville four days later was cancelled. Time for some rest and recuperation – well, no. Alice flew to New York for promotional duties, while the rest of the band were sent back to the Galesi Estate to work on material for the next album!

The next single was released on 27 March. 'No More Mr Nice Guy' had been Michael's choice for the first single and, in terms of chart positions, he was right as it did better than 'Hello Hooray', reaching number 25 in America.

Back on the tour, two 'home-town' shows at Detroit Cobo Hall in April were marked by a sensational achievement. The band were officially presented with platinum discs for sales of *Billion Dollar Babies*, an astonishing number of albums sold in just two months! The intensity of the stage show to support that album was being matched now by ever wilder audiences; at Chicago, Neal was hit in the back by a dart. The better news on 21 April came with *Billion Dollar Babies* hitting number one on the American album chart, the zenith perhaps of their career so far. That feat was equalled in Britain.

On 26 April, while in New Orleans for a show at the Memorial Auditorium, the band and management had a meeting which, according to *Creem* magazine, resulted in a decision to have a year off after the tour ended. That year off turned into barely a few months. Other plans that would have been discussed were the recording of some of the remaining dates of the tour for a film they had in production called *Good To See You Again*. Two shows were filmed in succession – Dallas Memorial Auditorium on 28 April and the Sam Houston Coliseum, Houston on 29 April. To the band's surprise, they were greeted at Houston airport by a film crew getting the shots for the Cowboys and Indians scene in the film. Everything about that scene was a surprise to them, including the content!

The fatigue from playing one-nighter after one-nighter on the tour was eased by that decision to hire the Starship. It meant they could use a base to fly in and out of and it was a top-class luxury airliner, with all the comforts you needed and more. Janice Buxton: 'I flew from Phoenix to Tucson (for the show at the Convention Center on 5 May) in their jet for a B$B show. That was the most turbulent 25 minutes of my life. Glen told me to sit in the bean bag chair and, 'Don't think about getting up!' I usually did what Glen said in safety situations!' Michael loved the Starship 'upgrade' but observed that, 'You know I never toured on a tour bus. We went from driving around in a nine-passenger station wagon to a DC3 jet and then a 707 – the Starship.'

Not so easily sorted were the problems with the audience throwing items on the stage. Alice was hit by a bottle at the Seattle show on 25 May, and to make things worse, he was also fined for disorderly conduct on-stage. By the time they reached New York's Madison Square Garden on 3 June Alice reported (in his autobiography) that he, 'Went on stage with six broken ribs, a fractured elbow and 20lb over-weight, bloated with fluid'. Warners pulled out all the stops to promote the Madison show, booking nineteen prime-time ten-second TV adverts on ABC. Warner's advertising director, Diana Balocca, explained to *Billboard* at the time that the aim was to, 'help maintain a state of grand frenzy in New York for the final concert of the Alice Cooper tour'. The show was recorded for possible use in the film.

Rather than finishing in New York, as planned, extra dates were added and the last show was on 7 June at Providence Civic Center in Rhode Island. The final encore was that run-through of 'Hard Day's Night', with Flo & Eddie joining in. With that, they were off, at last, the tour over. Also off were co-manager Joe Greenberg and lighting/props man Charlie Carnel, both leaving the organisation. Neal: 'Joe was 50% of the management team. We were doing our part as a band, and Joe and Shep were amazing, we all became really good friends. I can't say enough about

Joe. I used to call us the Magnificent Seven. We went from the ground floor to the top of the world'.

The tour left battered minds and bodies all round. Dennis: 'We were exhausted. We were lucky to get to bed by four in the morning; then we had to get up to catch an early flight or drive to the next city. But we had this keep-going-at-all-costs mentality that pulled us through.'

There was an unusual single release in June. The popularity of 'Halo Of Flies' with listeners to the Dutch off-shore radio station Veronica led to it being released in Holland and Belgium. This release came while plans for the band to tour Europe were still being rumoured, never confirmed or denied. Throughout June there had been publicity in the UK over attempts by the Welsh Labour MP Leo Abse to get the group banned from playing in the country. Abse told the press that his appeal to the Home Secretary, Robert Carr, to get the group banned started because of his teenage children's revulsion at the band's show. Joining Abse in his crusading moral stance was Mary Whitehouse of the National Viewers and Listeners Association.

While the band took some brief time off, Alice made his first stage appearance on his own. A 'Shakespearean Cabaret' was held at the Hollywood Bowl on 18 August featuring a host of stars raising money for a Free Shakespeare Festival to be held in Los Angeles. All of the performances were linked to Shakespeare in some way. Alice sang 'Gutter Cat Vs The Jets', which linked to *West Side Story* and thus to *Romeo And Juliet*. How the backing track was performed was not stated.

Warners put out the *School Days* double album in August, confusing any buyers expecting something akin to *Billion Dollar Babies,* and getting instead, a reissue of the band's first two albums. The cover did fit in with the recent releases – an illustration of Alice with a snake and the band around him, their four heads being from the David Bailey shoot re-drawn as illustrations. Opening up the gate-fold you got some shots from the Toronto 1969 gig and comments from Alice. It made it to an impressive number thirteen in the UK album chart.

The band regrouped in September, spending time working on tracks for *Muscle Of Love* at Sunset Sound Studios in Hollywood. According to Mick Mashbir the possibility of him being officially added to the band was under consideration:

It was in the works for a while. At one point there was supposed to be a secret test photo session with me and the band before Glen was due to show up for his band photos. He was always late, but on that day he was there early. Surprise! So, needless to say, it was a very short shoot. I don't recall if there were any actual photos of the band and me, but I got a cool one of just me out of it. Shep was trying to find a way to ease me into the picture, but he was very concerned with maintaining the image of the band. Glen was very popular and still is, with the fans of the ACG, so Shep was wary of making any changes without a way to hype me as the new guy. We met and talked about it a bit, and he said he would think of a way.

The new album's vocals were done in New York in October with a stellar cast of backing vocalists seen arriving at The Record Plant. *Muscle Of Love* was released on 20 November, keeping up the punishing album release schedule – their fifth new studio album since 1970's *Easy Action*. Tour rehearsals were conducted the same month at the Fillmore East in New York, as well as filming a promo video for 'Teenage Lament '74'.

The ensuing (confusingly named) 'Billion Dollar Babies Holiday Tour' to promote *Muscle Of Love* concentrated mostly on the northern American states and Canada. *Billion Dollar Babies* had been their biggest album to date and this meant they had to keep a solid number of songs from that album still in the set-list, so there was a look of familiarity about the running order. The *Muscle Of Love* tracks mostly got a mid-show focus. The set-list was: 'Hello Hooray', 'Billion Dollar Babies', 'Elected', 'I'm Eighteen', 'Big Apple Dreamin'', 'Muscle Of Love', 'Hard Hearted Alice', 'My Stars', 'Unfinished Sweet', 'Sick Things', 'I Love The Dead', 'School's Out', 'Working Up A Sweat'. Dropping 'No More Mr. Nice Guy' looks an odd decision, while 'My Stars' did get dropped on at least one date (New Haven Coliseum) where it was replaced by 'Dead Babies'. 'Working Up A Sweat' was the new encore, but a better option would have been to finish with' 'Muscle Of Love', a perfect final song. Neal remains a huge fan of their live performances of 'Muscle Of Love', 'I think it's the most powerful song that we do on stage even to this day'. A glaring omission in the set from the new album was the new single, 'Teenage Lament '74'. It could have been that the big vocal ending was felt unworkable, but more likely they felt it was too poppy for the set.

The tour kicked off on 8 December in Nashville. Supporting were Stories, who had had a number one single with their cover of Hot Chocolate's 'Brother Louie'. For all of the other dates on the tour, ZZ Top were the support, promoting their *Tres Hombres* album.

The Cooper Group played their set in the sailor suits familiar from the new album. Visually the show featured the same props, but the sarcophagus behind Neal was switched for a huge Christmas tree. The guillotine remained as the main feature (when possible). Cindy was back on stage as the dancing tooth and The Amazing Randi also returned. Beating up Nixon at the conclusion of the set was dropped, and replaced by the far more distasteful beating up of Santa Claus! Santa was portrayed by journalist Bob Greene, whose account of his time on tour with the band was to have repercussions later.

The violence that had bubbled up sporadically over both of the 1973 tours exploded at the show in Toledo, Ohio on 13 December. An element in the audience was out to cause trouble from the start, and as soon as the band came on they started hurling items at them. Alice was hit quite quickly during 'Hello Hooray', and after 'Billion Dollar Babies' the band decided to walk off until things calmed down. At this point, a cherry bomb was thrown onto the stage near Michael Bruce's position, reinforcing the decision to leave. The band didn't come back on and the gig was cancelled with a story put out to the press that Michael had been taken to hospital with a cut face and a piece of metal in his eye from where part of the lighting rig had broken in the explosion. This story, according to Bob Greene, was true in as much it was a crew member, not Michael, who had been hit and hurt badly.

Another problem during the tour was the snowy weather. A lot of the stage equipment didn't make it for three dates – Toronto, Syracuse and Norfolk – and the band had to work around the deficiencies which included the dentist drill and the guillotine. The drill was easy enough to work around and James Randi worked out how to do the execution with a sword instead. Also missing was the band's stage, which meant that the band were less 'confined' to the positions they were normally in on the chromed girders rig. It actually gave them more space to play together as a band and the musicians must certainly have welcomed that.

The tour finally wrapped up at Buffalo, New York on New Year's Eve, the end to a spectacular but gruelling year. It also marked the last gig by the band in America.

Billion Dollar Babies (Warner Bros.)

Personnel:
Alice Cooper: lead vocals, harmonica
Glen Buxton: lead guitar

Michael Bruce: guitar, backing vocals
Dennis Dunaway: bass, backing vocals
Neal Smith: percussion, backing vocals
with:
Donovan: vocals on 'Billion Dollar Babies'
Bob Ezrin: keyboards, mellotron, backing vocals on 'No More Mr. Nice Guy'
Steve Hunter: lead guitar solos on 'Generation Landslide', 'Billion Dollar Babies',
'Sick Things', 'Raped And Freezin'' and 'Unfinished Sweet'. Pedal steel on 'Hello
Hooray'
Will Jordan: broadcast voice on 'Elected'
Dave Libert: backing vocals
Al MacMillan: piano on 'Mary Ann'
Mick Mashbir: guitar on all except 'Elected', 'Generation Landslide', 'Sick Things'
and 'Mary Ann'
Jim Mason: backing vocals on 'No More Mr. Nice Guy'
Reggie Vincent: backing vocals, guitar on 'Raped And Freezin'', 'Billion Dollar
Babies', 'Elected' and 'No More Mr. Nice Guy'
Dick Wagner: lead guitar on 'I Love The Dead'
Dr. S. Wilk: dentist on 'Unfinished Sweet'
Produced at The Galesi Estate, Greenwich; The Record Plant, New York; Morgan
Studios, London, August 1972 – January 1973 by Bob Ezrin.
USA release date: 25 February 1973. UK release date: 24 March 1973
Highest chart places: USA: 1 UK: 1
Running time: 40:51

Alice explained to the Phoenix New Times in 2001 that: 'The whole idea
of *Billion Dollar Babies* was us sitting there saying, 'Two years ago, we
couldn't even buy a can of tuna fish. And people wouldn't let us play in
their bar for free. Now we're voted number-one band in the world above
the Beatles, above Led Zeppelin in *Melody Maker*, all those papers''.
　Mick Mashbir made his recording debut with the band on the album.
Getting the right sound at the Galesi Estate for his guitar proved an
unusual experience:

　　To isolate me and my rig from the rest of the band, I did my tracking
　　in the hat check room, which was basically a fancy closet. It was all
　　hardwood construction, hence the brightness of my sound on the
　　'Raped and Freezin'' and 'No More Mr Nice Guy' rhythm tracks. It was a
　　challenge to track in that space, having no one to vibe off of. The upside

was that there were no visual distractions. It's just me and the band in my headphones. It was a very personal, smokey, immersive experience.

Another guitar player added to the recording line-up was Steve Hunter. He told Jeb Wright of *Classic Rock Revisited* in 2012 that: 'I got the call from Bob to fly to New York to overdub on Alice's new album. I walked in the studio and there is Michael Bruce, Glen Buxton and Dennis Dunaway, and they were the coolest guys. I think I was called in because they wanted some different flavours on the album'. Who plays what, and where, has been the subject of conjecture over the years. Using the recollections of Michael Bruce, Mick Mashbir, Steve Hunter and Dick Wagner, we will address that as we look at each song.

Neal's percussion had grown over the years, reaching an apex on the 1973 albums and tours. 'There's different sections of the drum kit for different songs. From the big timbales to the floor toms, to the bongo drums, to the mounted toms in front of the snare drums, hi-hat and cymbals. Percussion is so deep.'

Added to the equipment used on the album was a mellotron. Michael: I remember the day we went out and found one and Bob played it and it was so cool, you know? We were living in Connecticut and we went somewhere upstate New York to this company that had it. They had a mellotron sitting there and Bob was just so excited'. You can hear Ezrin play the strings setting on it on 'Hello Hooray' and 'Unfinished Sweet'.

The music on the album represented an expansive step up from *School's Out,* and the cover was even more lavish. Ernie Cefalu:

> Our goal was always to make an album cover more than something that housed a record. An interactive thing that the fan got involved with more than just reading lyrics or credit or looking at pictures. I came up with the idea of the big wallet and the billion-dollar bill. Joe Petagno did the bill. Carl Ramsey, who was an airbrush illustrator, did the outer sleeve. My contribution was the concept, overseeing it and the lettering.

Also housed inside the snakeskin gatefold cover you found a set of trading card photographs of the band. The package was completed with a stunning David Bailey photograph of the band. Alice told *Classic Rock* in 2004 that: 'We used the best photographer, the guy we were sure was the guy in *Blow Up*, because we thought there was going to be models laying naked around the place, and there were a few'.

For Cindy Smith, the photo session meant a last-minute rush job: 'We were all looking forward to the David Bailey photo-shoot. We decided to do white satin suits for the shoot at the last minute.I made a list of supplies I needed and they magically appeared in our hotel room. Our room was small, but I made it work. I cut and sewed the suits for each guy, but the tricky part was fitting them. I finished Den's first, of course, because he was right there with me. The other guys were going in and out all night, so I'd grab them when I heard their voice and fit them. Sadly, I didn't make it to the shoot the next morning, I was asleep at the hotel, having stayed up all night sewing.'

Bailey's iconic photograph of the band with the rabbits, banknotes and a baby girl was initially rejected by Warners who asked for changes. Ernie Cefalu explains: 'They rejected it because of the baby. Alice is holding a baby girl and you could see her privates, so I came up with the idea of an oak leaf made out of one of the bills to cover them up'. The baby was band publicist Carolyn Pfeiffer's daughter Lola who later sadly died of cot death syndrome. Pfeiffer is thanked in the album credits along with industry mogul Clive Davis and, amusingly, Lawrence Talbot – the character name of the Wolf Man in 1940s horror movies.

The process of putting the album together was now well established. Bob Ezrin explained how it worked in 2001 to Serene Dominic of the *Phoenix New Times*:

We'd start by listening to the ideas that each of us had brought in. Basically, I was the arbiter, but everybody got to express themselves, and if something really grabbed our fancy, we'd pick up the instruments and start playing it. And that was a really good way to inspire creativity and freedom of thought. We would go to playing before we were ready to commit to anything. In the process, we worked up a lot of things that never got used, but part of them may have survived. It may have just been a riff, which we'd hold to the side until we needed another riff in D.

The sessions at Morgan Studios in London saw Robin Black engineering. 'He (Ezrin) had heard some Jethro Tull stuff I had done and wanted to come to the studio and work with me'. Robin found Ezrin to be, 'A very hands-on, powerful producer. Always very 'up', full of energy and he was very good at pushing to get the best result. The monitors were always flat out; Bob liked it loud to keep the live vibe up!'

Celebrity visitors regularly dropped in and a jam session featuring

Keith Moon, Marc Bolan, Rick Grech, Harry Nilsson and Flo & Eddie was recorded but remains unheard. It was apparently a drunken mess! Robin: 'Bob put a stop to it because it was taking away from recording the album'. More successful was a separate recording with Donovan, who popped in to share vocal duties on the title track. Robin was intrigued by the methods used to get the vocal takes down.

He brought in an eight-foot by four-foot mirror and Alice would be dressed up basically as he would be on-stage and he sang to himself in the mirror to psych himself up. I had never seen that before. He gave a performance and did all the expressions and body movements he might do on-stage. He did that for nearly every vocal we did.

After the Morgan sessions, the album was finished off in New York with guitar overdubs and orchestral sessions. Reggie Vincent isn't credited on the sleeve other than as a songwriter. So it may be his contributions were only for the preliminary sessions, or were cut in the final mixes.

The growing absence of Glen Buxton, combined with Bob Ezrin's growing influence, are among the reasons why it's not uniformly picked as their best album. Dennis is quick to point out that, 'Glen was there when we wrote most of what we wrote and he was the inspiration for a lot of songs'. While Michael feels that: '*Billion Dollar Babies* wasn't the best at representing the band. I think the best album lies somewhere between *Love It To Death* and *Killer*. The two of those together would be what I would call the original Cooper sound. *Billion Dollar Babies* turned into what *Welcome To My Nightmare* was for Alice'. He is absolutely right on that score but what they and Ezrin created with this album is a masterpiece. It's when their collective vision reached a peak, albeit at the expense of Glen Buxton and the smoothing out of their sound.

'Hello Hooray' (Rolf Kempf)

Alice told the *Phoenix New Times* in 2001 that the song's writer, Rolf Kempf, 'Was a friend of Bob Ezrin's. I was listening to it as the opening of the show and this was perfect. It had the kind of feel of 'Send in the Clowns'. I was thinking of it in a much bigger electrical way, but I loved the grandness of it'. The song left Neal Smith a little cold. 'It was the closest we got to doing that kind of song, but I would never have wanted to do it again. Any theatrics was fine, but to go and make the show a big song and dance thing like Broadway never appealed to me'.

Kempf's lyrical inspiration was the concept of self-renewal and re-invention. He told Robert Webb of *The Independent* that Alice had, 'Got the emotional essence of the tune right, and added a tag to bring it home'. Indeed he did, Alice added a lot to the lyrics, and they are mostly all his.

It was originally recorded by Judy Collins, the difference between her version and the one we know and love is quite dramatic. Ezrin does a great job of keeping the key instrumental features and building a huge wall of sound around them. 'Bob is the king of embellishments', agrees Michael. Ezrin's arrangement is majestic from the first notes, with a mellotron string effect prominent on the intro. Michael and Mick Mashbir handle the guitars on the bulk of this track. Listen carefully and there is an acoustic in the background playing the chords; it's easiest to hear on the choruses and is probably Michael playing.

Dennis recalls his bass part:

I keep playing the open A string underneath what I'm playing up there, so the bottom doesn't drop out. So I keep the low notes going while I'm playing up the neck. That took a little bit of creative thinking to do it that way, but it worked out great. A lot of people cite that song for the bass. On the opening line, I said I want the bass to sound more orchestrated. So we had Bob adding one piano note to double the bass, which made it sound so much bigger.

The build-up to the guitar solo is masterful, the tension builds and then, at 2:37, we get a pedal steel solo from Steve Hunter. The whole song is worth it just for that solo alone. How do you come up with a solo like that? Steve:

I brought a beat-up, mid-to late-50s Gibson six-string pedal steel to the sessions. Bob and I discussed the approach and settled on a solo and a harmony part. We plugged the Gibson into a Marshall half-stack, turned up the amp, and I worked out the solo. Then, I doubled the first half and played harmony to the second half. Over the chords immediately following the solo, I pushed a couple of the Gibson's 'chord pedals' to follow the progression. The tone was pretty organic – no effects pedals.

The end of the song is stunning with Alice's impassioned cries of 'God I feel so strong' ringing triumphantly over and over again as cannons go off in the distance. This epic opening track is a huge statement of intent – the drama and cinematic feel on the previous albums raised up several notches.

It was released as an edited single, backed with 'Generation Landslide'. It got to number six in the UK and number 35 in America.

'Raped And Freezin' (Bruce/Cooper)

Neal: 'We were recording songs as we were writing them. It was written and recorded in Greenwich in our mansion. There was usually a tape recorder running just so if we did something in a song we would remember it'.

A change of gears, and mood, with a track they would have trouble getting on an album today due to the lyrical matter. The twist is that it's Alice who is in trouble here, chasing off the lady, but that doesn't lessen the issues. If you can ignore the lyric issues what we have here is a crisp tight rocker with terrific guitar solos.

Mick Mashbir has vivid memories of recording this track.

My pre-chorus and chorus guitar fills were an obvious nod to Albert King, with a bit of George Harrison. That track was really rhythm-driven. Michael and I synched up really well. He's on the left channel and I'm on the right. When we were working it up, it wasn't really coming together. Then Ezrin stepped in with the rhythm track arrangement, and there you have it. It was pretty funny hearing a bunch of rockers playing the Samba outro. The solos were played by Michael and Steve Hunter, later at the Record Plant.

The solos kick in at 1:40 – the first sounds like Michael playing, with Steve Hunter taking the second straight after him at 1:55. Michael shares all the gloriously dirty rhythm guitar parts with Mick Mashbir.

Throughout, Ezrin plays a lively piano accompaniment that helps keep things light and airy. The songs ends in a joyous Mexican fiesta of carnival rhythms and distant cries of 'ole'. It was a highlight on the first 1973 tour, the band all gathered around Neal's drum riser like they were one unit again.

'Elected' (Cooper/Smith/Dunaway/Bruce/Buxton)

Given the subject matter, the song simply had to be a big production number. Bob Ezrin told the *Phoenix New Times* in 2001: 'It was, 'Why don't we run Alice for President as a joke?' We had 'Reflected', and we said, 'Why don't we just change the words?' Well, we can't exactly just change the words, but it was a good starting point'.

Famously Ezrin had Alice sing his vocals to a reflection of himself in a full-length mirror. This enabled Alice to build the performance element and 'sell' the song. In spite of the efforts to make it work Ezrin was never happy with the final mix (which took a week and allegedly cost a fortune), thinking he could have made it more punchy.

The song opens with Michael's crashing rhythm guitar and Neal's percussion. From there it's a succession of rolling rhythms with the bass melodically bubbling away in the mix. Ezrin goes for a solid wall of brass to augment the band throughout, while Alice's voice has reverb used on it to enhance the effect of him singing/speaking at a rally. From 2:51 to the fade is a series of unstoppable descending riffs, over which Alice proudly declaims, culminating in the memorable, 'Personally, I don't care!' It's a powerhouse of a track that, due to its origins from their earlier 'Reflected', clearly illustrates how far they have come since their first album.

It's possible that the song features Glen as the recording pre-dates his issues. There is no guitar solo in the song, but it could well be him, or maybe Reggie Vincent, on rhythm with Michael. The radio broadcaster voice is Will Jordan, impersonating the legendary Walter Winchell who had died in February 1972.

Alice told *Classic Rock* in 2004 of a proud moment:

Right after we cut 'Elected', I was at our record company office in New York, and John Lennon walked past me. He said, 'Great record, Alice'. I said, 'Thank you'. And then he took about three more steps and turned around and said, 'Paul would have done it better'. And I looked at him and went, 'Well, of course, he would – he's Paul McCartney!' But I was so thrilled. I mean, come on – John Lennon loved my song. It doesn't get any better than that.

The edited single version, backed with 'Luney Tune' from *School's Out,* got to number four in the UK, and number 26 in America. There is a major difference between the album and single versions. Alice's vocals are more prominent and in the centre of the sound spectrum on the single. On the album version, his vocals are placed over to the right and are less effective. It's also a different vocal take to the single.

'Billion Dollar Babies' (Cooper/Bruce/Reggie Vincent)
The song started with a tune cooked up by Reggie Vincent. Dennis:

He came in with this Roy Orbison-like ballad that was very beautiful that
he and Glen stayed up all night over. We had decided *Billion Dollar
Babies* would be the title of the album and there we were playing this
syrupy ballad and everybody's sitting down. Finally, I go, 'If this is going
to be the title track of the album we've got to put dynamite under our
seats'. So I jumped up and everybody said what have you got, but I
didn't really have anything. I just played da da da dah and then played it
again. 'It's got to be exciting', I said. That blew the whole ballad out of the
water right there. So I worked up the bass line and Ezrin said, 'OK, Alice
and Neal take a break while Dennis shows that riff to Glen and Michael'.
Then when they came back, Neal came up with the amazing drum part
and Alice changed the lyrics, so there was nothing left of that ballad. But
would all that have happened if Reggie hadn't come in with the song? I
don't know.

Neal Smith's iconic flam stroke drum intro stuns to this day. He is often
heard to say that no drummer since him has ever played it 'right'. He may
not get a song-writing credit for it but without his intro, and indeed his
playing throughout it, it wouldn't be anything like the same song. The
skipping rhythms are such a huge part of the sound. Neal: 'I wanted to
play something that was really me. Bob said I could try it, but I had better
play it perfect and I did'. That intro must have sent ripples across the rock
music world in 1973; it was, and still is, so inventive and innovative.

The droning intro guitars are Michael and Mick Mashbir, with Mick
also handling the lead fills that pepper the song – those little accents
that pop in around the choruses. The first guitar solo, at 1:20, is Michael,
leading into Steve Hunter at 1:30. The overlap here and the effect of the
two trading solos are simply stunning. Steve pops up again at 2:50 with a
longer solo all the way through to the fade-out.

Asking Donovan to sing lead with Alice was a clever idea. The duo
trade vocals with Donovan using the top of his register and sounding
all the more manic for it. It makes for good contrast with Alice, helping
to conjure up a schizophrenic personality at work and play. Donovan
told *Classic Rock* in 2001 that, 'He was downstairs and I was upstairs at
Morgan Studios. I had heard this track and he asked me to put a vocal on
it and I said, 'Sure. But it's so big and so bouncy and so loud, I think I'm

going to have to get into a falsetto!' No one believed it was me!'

The 'nightly in the attic' section is darkly delicious with the dancing melody providing a contrast to the song's main structure. Fans of The Hollies would recognise the melody from their 'Tell Me To My Face', which came out in 1966. A sub-conscious borrowing here!

An edited version was released as a single in America, backed with 'Mary Ann', which must be the most unusual choice of B-side ever selected for the band or Alice. The single got to number 57 on the charts.

'Unfinished Sweet' (Cooper/Bruce/Smith)

Searching for inspiration, an idea hit Alice. In 2001 he explained to *Classic Rock* that: 'I was trying to think of the worst sound in the world – a dentist drill. We've got to get that thing in there because I would love to do a thing on stage with a giant dentist drill. How horrible is that? Tap into that fear. Everyone hates that'.

This big production feature track starts off with Alice complaining about problems with his teeth and finally making that trip to the dentist. Apparently, he did this for real to get the sound effects. The originally planned, but cut, intro voice saying 'Have you ever had gas before?' turned up on the *NME* flexi-disc. Sequence it yourself at the beginning of this track and it works superbly. Instead it opens with a Dennis intro with those scraping bass notes, with Neal joining followed by the twin rhythm guitars of Michael and Mick Mashbir.

As the gas kicks in and Alice slumbers uneasily, his mind (and the music) drifts. Neal: 'I love it when it goes into the whole thing where the patient has a James Bond dream'. While Dennis keeps up a bubbling riff, Mick Mashbir cranks out the 'James Bond Theme'. The orchestral part adding the high wash in the background here is Bob Ezrin on the mellotron. After Mick finishes, Michael takes the next solo, before Mick again returns with the 'Bond Theme'. The ominous shaking sounds which follow, as the tooth is coming out, are Dennis playing a wah-wah pedal on the bass.

The tooth extraction is triumphantly followed by a jubilant four-note riff played by what sounds like the entire band in unison. The Mellotron part here gives a clue as to where this was borrowed from – it's a straight homage to the section in Tchaikovsky's '1812 Overture' just before the rousing end section starts with the cannons.

The song picks back up with some seriously funky drumming from Neal with what sounds like (ironically) a jaw harp bouncing along. Neal finally turns it around with a killer drum roll, kicking the tempo up for the final verse. The dual rhythm guitars are back and this is a really mean and dirty ending. The outro comprises sublime chiming guitars as Alice feels the pain. All this and a false ending too, marvellous stuff! The boys were ahead of the game with this track; three years later the terror of the dentist was brought home again in the film *Marathon Man.*

'No More Mr. Nice Guy' (Bruce/Cooper)
Michael rightly regards this as one of his best songs:

> I wrote it originally back when we were doing *Killer*. The lyrics were different – 'I used to be such a sweet, sweet thing, but that was just a burn. I used to break my back to kiss her ass and got nothing in return. All my friends told me, man; you are crazy for being such a fool. But I guess I was 'cause being in love, made me so uncool'. When we looked at it again, Alice changed the words around so it was about him. He re-wrote the chorus and came up with some good lyrics.

In 2001 Alice told *Classic Rock* that:

> It was pretty much based after 'Substitute' (by The Who), the most pop record we ever did. It was kind of an in-joke for us. Everybody at that point didn't know whether to hate us or love us. But I was definitely, with the general public, the worst person ever. I was the Antichrist; I was everything. And I said, 'Okay, that does it. Gloves are off – No More Mr. Nice Guy. Now we're gonna get rough'.

But where did the title come from? Back in 1971 Sparks (then called Half Nelson) released their debut album and the last track was 'No More Mr. Nice Guys'. Joseph Fleury, Sparks' manager, added an intriguing extra detail to Sparks' biographer Dave Thompson. 'Alice Cooper originally contacted us to ask if they could borrow a lyric from one of Ron Mael's other songs, 'Beaver O'Lindy' – 'I'm the girl in your head, and the boy in your bed'. We politely declined and the next thing we knew they had taken the title from 'Nice Guys' without even asking'.

It remains one of the band's most popular and classic songs. Mick Mashbir's harmony guitars when Alice is singing are just sublime, a sweet tone to them without being overly so. The delicate slides Mick makes into the choruses are a treat too. Underneath the lead parts, the counterpoint of Michael's choppy rhythm playing gives the track some bite. Dennis's slides up and down the frets are stunning on the track and Neal keeps things ticking over beautifully.

Mick had travelled with the band on a few dates of the 1972 European tour before returning to Blakes, their London hotel. While waiting for the band to arrive back to record, he kept busy:

I got Warners to send me a tape recorder and the basic tracks. Then I got the dreaded London flu of '72. While I was delirious from the flu, I came up with parts for different songs, including the lead lines for 'No More Mr Nice Guy'. The band returned from their tour dates, and we went into Morgan Studios to track more and overdub. I had my parts prepared and with some arrangement suggestions from Bob Ezrin, the overdubs were completed in a fairly short time. I used an Ampeg VT-22 and my strat for all the overdubs.

A last-minute inclusion were the backing vocals featuring Jim Mason, who only popped in to meet Bob Ezrin for dinner:

I was producing a project in Studio B, and down the hall in Studio A, Bob Ezrin was mixing B$B. We both worked for Nimbus 9 Productions, and we had planned to have dinner together that evening. I finished my session around six pm and wandered into Bob's session. 'He was just finishing the mix on 'No More Mr. Nice Guy'. He played it for me and asked, 'What do you think?' I said I liked the mix, but where were the background vocals? His response was, 'There are none. Do you think there should be?' My answer, 'Yes', was met with, 'Sing me what you hear'. So I did. Bob's response was a big grin, and, 'Hell yes!' He set up a vocal mic and recorded my ideas for the chorus, 'No more mr. nice guy, no more mr. clea-ee-ee-ean'. Then he and I added some additional parts, 'Nice guy ohh', which he added into a new mix. By now, both hungry, we headed out for dinner. After dinner, Bob suggested that I come back to the studio with him because Alice and Shep were coming over to hear what mixes he had completed. When they heard 'Nice Guy', I remember Alice's response was, 'Cool, who's that singing with me?' 'That's Mason', said Bob. 'It's both of us', I added. 'Nice', said Alice, tossing me a can of Budweiser, which he always seemed to have in hand. That was my singular contribution to that project. They were kind enough to include my name in the album credits, but I can't recall if I was ever paid, although Bob did pay for dinner!

It was released as a single backed with 'Raped And Freezin''. It got to number ten in the UK, while in America it reached number 25.

'Generation Landslide' (Cooper/Bruce/Dunaway/Smith/Buxton)

'I see them as the best lyrics I have ever written. I remember sitting down and writing them as a flow of consciousness in the Canary Islands. I was leaning against a wall, with a pen and a piece of paper, while a big lightning storm went on, and twenty minutes later there it was', Alice explained to *Classic Rock* in 2001. What he does in the lyrics is to write a summary of America at that time, to which the album acts as a kind of mirror.

The band had been one song short for the album and were sent off to the Canary Islands to get some rest, and write the song. Alice delivers the lyrics in a stream of consciousness, almost rap style, while Neal and Dennis hammer out the driving beat. Neal: 'I started playing the drum beat and Michael joined in. We had the song basically written in a couple of days, everyone participated in its creation'. For the band, it was back to old times in terms of how they worked up a song. A real ensemble piece that shows off their combined strengths. Dennis says it's his favourite on the album. 'It's one of those songs where everybody put in ideas and we would try everybody's out. That was the rule, you can't shoot down somebody's idea unless you've given it a heartfelt honest try. Then we would take a vote and the majority would win. There would be no looking back and everybody would go full tilt ahead and that worked really well for us'.

It's Glen playing the spoons on the intro to the track, which he does marvellously. The rhythm guitar part is also possibly Glen, but if not it means all the guitar is by Michael except the solo.

The instrumental break, with great harmonica from Alice, segues into that classic soaring guitar solo from Steve Hunter, the lyricism in his playing is fabulous. It's a remarkable piece of work and one that Bob Ezrin highlighted as a magic moment when he wrote the sleeve notes for Steve's solo album called *The Deacon*.

'Generation Landslide' is the best track on the album, and right up there as one of their best songs full stop.

'Sick Things' (Ezrin/Cooper/Bruce)

Bob Ezrin was the driving force on this one and explained in 2001 to *Classic Rock* that 'It's supposed to sound like the whole universe has slowed down to half speed. Some of the stuff was actually recorded at a higher speed and slowed down to normal'. Opening with deep shaking bass notes and Alice's sinister vocals, it is ahead of its time. A brass orchestral score, courtesy of Ezrin, works well in the soundscape, but the overall effect is somehow still of a minimal arrangement. The rhythm guitar parts, very low in this mix, are all handled by Michael.

The instrumental break starts off with pure noise and features what is generally agreed to be one of Glen's only three appearances on the album. It's him smashing the guitar in this section. With Steve Hunter making another startling appearance (at 3:32) for the solo, in which he plays the blues, a spaced out take on the genre that glides down into the opening piano notes of 'Mary Ann'. It's a beautifully constructed solo that features most of the melodic part of the song's construction.

Also in that 2001 *Classic Rock* feature, Alice explained that he had not been too sure about the inclusion of the song on the album. 'It's so creepy; it belonged on one of the creepier albums. Lyrically, it fits right in there. I was thinking about the fans. We were always kind of making fun of us and our fans. Our fans were fans, but they were cultish. I mean, even to this day there are people today who are absolutely frightening cultish fans'.

Creepy it definitely is and that vocal track has to be heard to be believed. Alice sounds like he is possessed by demons, or perhaps it's the coaxing words of a serial killer. Either way, this is the most unsettling vocal he has ever done.

'Mary Ann' (Bruce/Cooper)

If 'Sick Things' had segued into' I Love The Dead' it would have made perfect sense. But the idea to break the tension up with this cabaret piece works, somehow accentuating the feeling of unease. You must be missing something, there must be a twist, but the twist is that there isn't one other than the final, 'I thought you were my man.'

It's a minimal piece musically as, apart from Alice, there is only Al MacMillan (uncredited on the sleeve, but confirmed by Michael) on piano. As well as accompanying Alice, he is given the extended outro alone to show his considerable chops. It's hard to dislike the song, but it's also hard to avoid feeling it is the filler it was obviously intended to be.

The song's origins were in a Michael Bruce demo called 'Uncle Sam', which was a Vietnam War protest song. The original vibe was, says Michael, 'Almost a Lady Madonna type thing. But I didn't write it thinking it was going to be on the album'. Alice re-wrote the words and instead, we have a brief reflective note to a friend or lover, or even Mary Whitehouse – whom Alice claimed as an 'inspiration'. It's unknown if she ever knew that 'Mary Ann' was pointedly named to infuriate her.

'I Love The Dead' (Ezrin/Cooper/Wagner)

Alice also said that he felt this song too doesn't necessarily fit on the album. It does point strongly towards *Welcome To My Nightmare* – no surprise given the trio involved in its creation. The sleeve doesn't credit Dick Wagner as co-writer. He sold his writing credit for $6,000, and got paid $90 for playing on it! Michael plays all the rhythm guitar parts and says he too was involved in writing the song, specifically the music on the unexpectedly positive chorus!

A sparkling piano by Ezrin opens the track, along with Neal's gentle cymbal work. His drums and Dennis's bass enter and up the tempo, as we cut to the graveyard where Alice waits for us. The instrumentation remains sparse and understated; only an attractive three-note descending guitar punctuates the mood. Alice turns in a crepuscular vocal performance that both draws you in, and repulses, with the lyrics. The music builds with Dick Wagner handling the howling lead guitar parts that echo the horror in the lyrics.

The choruses are sickeningly catchy, building up to a big vocal ending. Anybody who was around who could sing seems to be on for backing vocals. At 4:08, if you strain your ears, someone riffs on the vocal melody intro from The Marcels' song 'Blue Moon'. That big choral section also marks the only appearance of Glen Buxton on the track, whose orgasmic groans were hopefully recorded in the studio.

Finally, there is no escape – 'cadaver eyes upon me see (jagged cut noises) nothing'. And that's how you finish a number one album.

Related Songs
'Coal Black Model T' (Cooper/Dunaway)

A demo and similar to the finished cut that became 'Slick Black Limousine'. They were right to change the car and the title as that works much better than this less 'slick' demo!

'Hard Day's Night' (John Lennon/Paul McCartney)

This was only performed live once, on the *Billion Dollar Babies* tour. The last night was on 7 June 1973 at Providence in Rhode Island, and after the usual encore, the band came back, along with Flo & Eddie, and ran through a ragged but enthusiastic version of the Beatles song. Fortunately, it was recorded in low-fi quality and is fairly easy to find. It is worth hearing because of it being the last song on the tour and a celebration of their feat in pulling it all off.

'School's Back In' (Cooper/Bruce/Buxton/Dunaway/Smith)

This was due to come out in 2017 when an archive release of the *School's Out* album was being prepared. Dennis: 'It's a song that we did in the studio, warming up and jamming. We decided if we wrote a song called 'School's Back In' then it would have to be the most depressing blues song ever. It is so depressing that there is a big build like it's going to the next chord change, but it goes back to the same chord'. Neal remembers that 'We did a version of it as we were getting a sound-check in Morgan Studios while we were recording *Billion Dollar Babies*. To this day Michael still plays a slow version of 'I'm Eighteen' ('Forever Eighteen'), which musically is exactly that song'. Sadly any archive reissue of it is still on the shelf.

'Slick Black Limousine' (Cooper/Dunaway)

This out-take from the sessions was given away with the *NME* as one side of a flexi-disc. The other side had excerpts from the forthcoming album. Amusingly the song starts with a false ending before kicking back in with a rockabilly rhythm from Neal and Dennis. Alice's Elvis-styled vocal gives the game away that we have a full-on Sun Records-style rocker. The song shifts gears at 1:45 and Mick Mashbir cranks out some very T. Rex-style riffs. He also added the creamy slide licks to the mix. Meanwhile, Alice is turning on his Elvis voice big-style.

It all gets very surreal with the ga-ga-ga backing vocals, but the band hold down the relentless rhythm and keep things ticking over. Dennis: 'On the ending when it goes into the weird Fellini-like part, that's another one of those parts which Neal and I would often warm ourselves up playing'. Could it have fitted on the album? Maybe not, there's only 'Mary Ann' you could see it replacing. What it would have been was a perfect B-side.

'Son Of Billion Dollar Babies' (Cooper/Bruce/Dunaway/Smith/Buxton)

This demo for 'Generation Landslide' shows the band working on the key elements of the track. Alice sings a guide vocal to work out the meter of the words, but gets in some of the inflexions he knows he will be using.

Glen's spoons are more apparent on the intro and it's feasible they were edited into the released track from this demo.

Archive releases
Billion Dollar Babies (Deluxe Edition CD)

This came out in 2001 as a digipack double CD release from Rhino. A remastered upgrade of the original album is on disc one, while disc two had the two demos plus 'Slick Black Limousine' and an incomplete live set from 1973.

The live set covers the same concerts as the *Good To See You Again* film, but does not necessarily feature the same versions as used in the film.

Billion Dollar Babies (Quad Mix Vinyl)

The fad in the '70s for quad music systems saw some best-selling albums produced for the market. What we know about the quad mix of *Billion Dollar Babies* comes from listening to it, and a reference in Bob Greene's book when Shep Gordon asks Jack Richardson if the quad mix will be ready for the end of November. Jack was working on *Muscle Of Love* at the Record Plant at the time so it makes sense that he would have gone on to work on this remix.

The quad mix is just over two minutes longer, with significant differences to listen out for. The version you are likely to come across is a fold-down in stereo resulting in Alice's vocals getting pushed higher in the sound spectrum. Several tracks are extended with longer fade-outs. 'Hello Hooray' and 'Raped And Freezin'' both feature noticeably different vocal takes and the latter benefits from a longer outro.

The big changes come on the outro of 'Generation Landslide', where the lead guitar, after a longer, extended ending, falls apart and echoes into prolonged slow drum beats, which segue into 'Sick Things'. The latter's intro also has a prominent rhythm guitar part by Michael restored to the mix. When we get to the end of 'Sick Things' (which is 40 seconds longer than the standard version), it segues right into 'Mary Ann' – no gap on this version. 'Mary Ann' now opens with the clinking of glass and laughter in a bar which heighten the lounge bar feel of the track.

The changes in particular to these tracks make for an intriguing extended side two. The new sound effects and more liberal use of channel panning (the guitar solo on 'Sick Things' swaps channels at dizzying pace for example) was undoubtedly to heighten the surround sound mix. Lots then to enjoy here for Cooper connoisseurs.

Right: Alice onstage in London or Glasgow in 1972. (*NME Annual 1973*)

Below: Alice and Vincent Price in a promo shot for 'The Nightmare'. (*Rhino*)

Bottom: Cindy Smith, Dennis Dunaway and Michael Bruce relax at the hotel in 1972. (*Len DeLessio*)

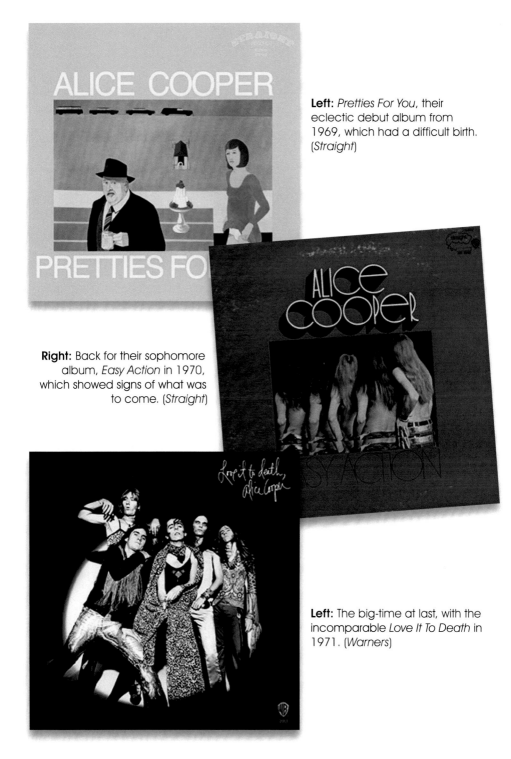

Left: *Pretties For You*, their eclectic debut album from 1969, which had a difficult birth. (*Straight*)

Right: Back for their sophomore album, *Easy Action* in 1970, which showed signs of what was to come. (*Straight*)

Left: The big-time at last, with the incomparable *Love It To Death* in 1971. (*Warners*)

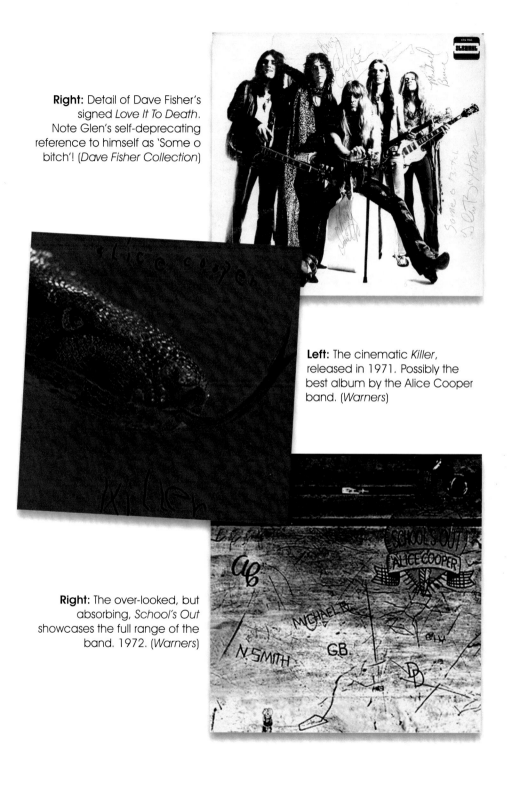

Right: Detail of Dave Fisher's signed *Love It To Death*. Note Glen's self-deprecating reference to himself as 'Some o bitch'! (*Dave Fisher Collection*)

Left: The cinematic *Killer*, released in 1971. Possibly the best album by the Alice Cooper band. (*Warners*)

Right: The over-looked, but absorbing, *School's Out* showcases the full range of the band. 1972. (*Warners*)

Above: The terrific front cover of the *Killer* tour programme. Another shot from the sessions for the album. (*Pete Turner*)

Right: Dennis Dunaway in the spotlight from the *Killer* tour programme.

Left: Michael Bruce gets the harmony parts in. From the *Killer* tour programme.

Left: Sticks flying. Neal Smith from the *Killer* tour programme.

Right: Alice onstage in 1971. From the *Killer* tour programme.

Right: The late, great Glen Buxton takes a solo, From the *Killer* tour programme.

Below: The band at the front door of the Galesi Estate, their home and in-house rehearsal and recording studio. From the *Killer* tour programme.

Left: Top of the charts for *Billion Dollar Babies*, their biggest and most lavish album yet, 1973. (*Warners*)

Right: The original band's last album came packaged in a box, *Muscle Of Love*, 1973. (*Warners*)

ATTENTION:
THIS CARTON CONTAINS ONE (1)
ALICE COOPER
MUSCLE OF LOVE

FRAGILE

Left: Alice steps out alone for *Welcome To My Nightmare*, 1975. (*Atlantic*)

Right: *Alice Cooper Goes To Hell* reflected some new musical trends and was his most diverse album yet. 1976. (*Warners*)

Left: 1977's *Lace And Whisky* lacked consistency, but still has its moments. (*Warners*)

Right: *From The Inside* in 1978 was a partial return to form, but the album was over-produced. (*Warners*)

Right: 'Bodies need their rest'. 'Black Juju' at Copenhagen in 1971. (*Author collection*)

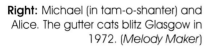

Left: Donovan, Alice, Glen and Bob Ezrin take a break at Morgan Studio in 1972. (*Author collection*)

Right: Michael (in tam-o-shanter) and Alice. The gutter cats blitz Glasgow in 1972. (*Melody Maker*)

Right: 'School's Out' at the Hollywood Bowl in 1972. (*Nightmare Returns tour programme*)

Below: Alice on the *Welcome To My Nightmare* tour in 1975 (*Author collection*)

Above: The *Nightmare* band. Top: Prakash John, Pentti Glan and Jozef Chirowksi. Bottom: Steve Hunter and Dick Wagner. (*Rolling Stone*)

Right: John Tropea's talents are all over *Goes To Hell*. (*John Tropea*)

Left: Allan Schwartzberg (centre) and his pal Jimmy Maelen (right) play on *Goes To Hell* and *Lace And Whiskey*. (*Allan Schwartzberg*)

Right: Alice as private eye Maurice Escargot on the inside of *Lace And Whiskey*. (*Warners*)

Left: Alice, with Steve Hunter behind him, on the Madhouse Rock tour, 1979. (*Madhouse Rock tour programme*)

Below: Alice with little Betty in the pram for 'Dead Babies' in 1979. (*Madhouse Rock tour programme*)

Right: The best Greatest Hits album ever? Absolutely it is! It was released in 1974. (*Warners*)

Left: Alice deserved a better live album than *The Alice Cooper Show* from 1977 and, frankly, so did we. (*Warners*)

Right: A David Bailey shot, as featured inside *Billion Dollar Babies* and signed by Alice. (*Warners*)

Kinetic Circus Mayfair,
Bull Ring, Birmingham, 021-643 2137   № T 0380
Doors open 8 p.m.

THURSDAY, 4th NOVEMBER

A L I C E
C O O P E R

Admission Ticket

Left:A ticket for the Birmingham Kinetic Circus gig in 1971, Signed by the band. Michael signed the back! (*Dave Fisher collection*)

John Smith Productions Ltd
present

ALICE COOPER

in Green's Playhouse

Fri. 10th November at 8

STALLS £1.50

H

№   38

No ticket exchanged

To be given up

Above: Ticket for the legendary Green's Playhouse gig at Glasgow in 1972. (*Author collection*)

Above right: A fully signed note-holder inside *Billion Dollar Babies*. This was given to the author by a former member of the roadcrew. (*Author collection*)

Right: The author with Dennis Dunaway, Neal Smith and Michael Bruce at Sickcon in Crewe in 2002. (*Phil McMullen*)

Billion Dollar Babies (DVD Audio)

This is notable for featuring a 5.1 mix produced by Bob Ezrin. The album comes alive more than ever with this mix, which is subtly spread around five speakers. The one big difference is that the alternate take of 'Raped And Freezin'' (as heard on the quad mix) is used instead.

Bonus features include the full promo video of 'Elected' (complete with the brief often cut bombs dropping sequence) and five of the live tracks from the deluxe edition of the album, recorded at Sam Houston Coliseum, Texas on 28 April. These five – 'Hello Hooray', 'Billion Dollar Babies', 'Elected', 'No More Mr Nice Guy' and 'I Love The Dead' – are also mixed in 5.1 and sound way better than on the deluxe edition.

This attractive package is completed with the original stereo mix in higher resolution.

Good To See You Again (DVD And Blu-ray)

The sketches wear thin quickly, other than the stage wrecking ending to 'The Lady Is A Tramp'. As the band destroy that hideous set, Alice's impassioned cry of 'Build our stage, build OUR stage' gives me goosebumps every time.

Happily, the core of the film is a full live set compiled from two or three dates on the *Billion Dollar Babies* tour. The filming is murky at times, and there is nowhere near enough footage of the rest of the band (it's very Alice focused) but is still superb – a gripping performance. What hits you straight away is the energy the band puts into the live performances. The dive-bombing descent from 'Elected' into 'I'm Eighteen', for example, is absolutely magnificent. Michael: 'We come on and give them a taste with 'Hello Hooray', then we get to rock it!' Neal: 'Recording in the studio is a whole different mind-set. We would speed everything up on stage because we were trying to drive the audience into a frenzy. Whatever it took to get the audience ripped and roaring we would do it. I was listening to the live version of 'Hello Hooray' and I don't even know how the hell I played it. It's so fast, but it's precise and straight on'.

Among those who loved seeing the show in the flesh was Jonny Podell: 'I wasn't originally (a fan) but quickly got sold and I watched more shows as a fan than any of my other clients.'

Billion Dollar Babies Live (Vinyl)

This Record Store Day release came as a 12" vinyl album with a bonus single. The cover says all of the tracks were recorded at the Houston 1973 show, but listening comparisons with other available recordings suggest 'Unfinished Sweet' and the single of 'School's Out'/'Under My Wheels' are from Dallas 1973.

Over the span of the album and single you get a full set, minus the taped filler tracks. It's a great live document of the band on this tour, though a lot of the audio is also on the *Good To See You Again* film soundtrack. It was a limited edition release.

Muscle Of Love (Warner Bros.)

Personnel:
Alice Cooper: lead vocals
Glen Buxton: lead guitar
Michael Bruce: guitar, backing vocals
Dennis Dunaway: bass, backing vocals
Neal Smith: percussion, backing vocals
with:
Mick Mashbir: lead guitar
Bob Dolin: keyboards, synthesiser, backing vocals
and:
Stanley 'the Baron' Behrens: harmonica on 'Working Up A Sweat'
Paul Prestopino: banjo on 'Crazy Little Child'
Jack Richardson: squeeze drum on 'Muscle Of Love'
Dick Wagner: lead guitar on 'Big Apple Dreamin'' and 'Working Up A Sweat'
Al MacMillan: string and brass arrangements
Allan Schwartzberg: drums on 'Crazy Little Child'
Reggie Vincent: backing vocals (uncredited)
Nona Hendryx & Sarah Dash: backing vocals on 'Teenage Lament '74'
Liza Minnelli: backing vocals on 'Teenage Lament '74' and 'Man With The Golden Gun'
The Pointer Sisters: backing vocals on 'Teenage Lament '74' and 'Working Up A Sweat'
Ronnie Spector: backing vocals on 'Teenage Lament '74'
Stu Daye, Joe Gannon, Dennis Ferrante and Dave Libert: backing vocals
Produced at Sunset Sound, Hollywood; The Record Plant, New York; The Galesi Estate, Greenwich, September – October 1973 by Jack Richardson and Jack Douglas.
USA release date: 20 November 1973. UK release date: 12 January 1974
Highest chart places: USA: 10, UK: 34
Running time: 39:31

On 25 May 1973, the band were in a limousine heading for the Center Coliseum, Seattle trying to come up with a better title for the album than 'A Kiss And A Fist'. Neal: 'Ideas and titles were flying around and Glen, who was lying on the floor and hadn't said anything till then, says *Muscle Of Love,* and that was the one. I love that title.'

Although it was very successful, the sales figures showed a dip after the all-conquering success of *Billion Dollar Babies* and this was probably another factor in the band's eventual fragmentation.

The absence of any input from Glen Buxton is a huge loss, as he would have given the songs some of his customary edge, and more of the jazz he loved. Dennis concurs: 'The problem with the continuity on *Muscle Of Love* is because Glen wasn't on it. If Glen had been on it would have sounded more like an Alice Cooper album'. Michael points out that, 'We did try to get Glen back on *Muscle Of Love,* but it didn't happen, and it's unfortunate that album didn't do as well'.

Glen was, however, around in the initial stages of putting the songs together. Mick Mashbir: 'They decided to make sure GB was involved in the writing process, like the old days, so they had band writing sessions that I wasn't allowed to attend. Mike Bruce and I shared a house with a studio, so we would work on the new tunes together'. Michael: 'I was writing a lot of music as I always did, but that's what I do!'

Dick Wagner also returned, brought in by co-producer Jack Richardson. Thanks to Mick, Dick and Michael Bruce the guitar parts will be credited for each song in the reviews.

Along with Glen, Bob Ezrin's absence is also keenly felt. There are great songs, but the lack of his typical production gloss is noticeable. Despite this, Michael still felt that there was enough continuity to keep things on an even keel. 'As a producer, Jack Richardson was about as close as you could get to Bob Ezrin. He had worked on *Love It To Death* and *Killer.* So to my thinking, it wasn't about what went wrong with *Muscle Of Love* as what didn't go right.'

Bob Ezrin had turned up intending to do the album, but things quickly turned sour. The band were running through songs in the rehearsal studio when Bob arrived. Michael: 'We were playing 'Big Apple Dreamin'' and he started correcting us and he didn't even say hello. He wasn't very gentlemanly-like, although he did have things going on in his life'. Words were exchanged and Ezrin left, never to return. An interesting perspective comes from Jack Douglas, who took over the production role with Jack Richardson. He told John Manulis of *Ageist* in 2019 that he had been asked to take on the role by Ezrin. 'He said, "I don't want to do it. It's the last Alice album with the band and I don't like funerals; I don't want to be there."' Excited by his opportunity, Douglas shared the news with his friend John Lennon, who asked where they were going to record the album. 'Wherever they tell me to do it', said Douglas. To which Lennon countered, 'No. Here's the thing, you're the producer now, you tell them where you want to do it'.

It's apparent from the opening bars of 'Big Apple Dreamin' that things are different. More understated than the usual big dramatic opener, but it still works because it's a great song. More problematic is the inclusion of so many iconic female vocalists doing back-ups. They're all terrific in their own right, but the way they are used here leaves them sounding anonymous. It could be any accomplished singer on back-ups. Surely it would have made better sense to have used one or two of them in a more strongly featured capacity?

As for the packaging concept, the idea of putting the album inside a cardboard box was a novel idea. Combined with the title stamped in pink, it suggested some exciting content hidden inside. The box though proved a problem as it was difficult for retailers to fit many in the racks and it wasn't robust. Some also thought the greasy stain on the front wasn't meant to be there and sent copies back.

Inside the box, there are great shots on the record sleeve of the band as sailors on shore leave visiting the Institute Of Nude Wrestling. Ernie Cefalu: 'That was the front of our offices. We painted it to look like a mud wrestling place because that was really big at the time. The plain wrapper cardboard box was so you wouldn't know what was in it. The grease stain at the bottom was to suggest that what was in there had broken, leaking out the bottom'.

We first see the band outside 'The Institute' eager to get in, then overleaf thrown out in disarray. One final image has them peeling a mountain of potatoes as penance for their infractions. Ernie: 'We wanted to put them on KP because they were AWOL so they got penalised. So we put them in the kitchen, but we didn't have any money to build the set. So somebody said, you know the Scientologists have a big ship in the San Pedro harbour, so we set it all up and we went down there. We put the band in the Galley'.

An additional curiosity was the credits insert which contained baffling instructions on how to fold it up as a book cover! Once you got past all of this there was the album, their most eagerly awaited one yet – the follow-up to a number one hit.

A quadraphonic mix, by Jack Richardson, was released with little difference to the stereo version. Alice adds a line about 'the birds and the bees' in 'Muscle Of Love' and the synthesiser part from Bob Dolin on 'Man With The Golden Gun' gets a welcome boost in the mix, but that is about it.

'Big Apple Dreamin' (Hippo)' (Bruce/Buxton/Cooper/Dunaway/Smith)

It was slated to be the first single because, as Dennis explains: 'At that time record companies always wanted the single to be the first song on the album'. It also has to be placed as side one track one because of the lyrics, which sees some guys from Ohio looking forward to the delights of New York, which are then dealt with as a series of vignettes in the remaining tracks. The Hippo was a nightclub frequented by the band, which explains why the song sleazily grooves along on a shuffling, almost disco beat. Neal and Dennis are superb here, the two playing in the pocket, but Dennis is not so happy with it. 'That's never been my favourite to play because I locked into such a standard pattern of groove on it. I don't do what I normally do'. Michael's raw rhythm guitar riffs anchor the track with Bob Dolin's organ layering up the sound. Mick Mashbir takes the guitar solo at 1:16 and then Dick Wagner comes in at 2:01, subtly at first, but he then adds counterpoint guitar fills to Alice's vocals, which sound like they are duelling together. A violin adds colour throughout the song, throwing in a repeated refrain that references George Gershwin's 'Rhapsody In Blue', subtly adding to the New York feel.

The song builds up to a long ending with Dick Wagner soloing away while Alice gets ever more urgent in his pledges to New York that they are coming to see what it's made of. As the song fades, unexpectedly the focus shifts and that violin gets a solo that picks up on the wistfulness in the lyrics. Who was that violinist? Sadly he isn't credited and nobody seems to know his or her name.

'Never Been Sold Before' (Bruce/Buxton/Cooper/Dunaway/Smith)

The subject of this song is sick of life as a New York prostitute, sick of the pimp who takes the money and sick of the likes of our Ohio boys on their way into the city. While the song is credited to all the band, Mick Mashbir asserts that he wrote a lot of the music, such as the verse parts. Mick:

While we were rehearsing in Toronto for *MOL*, I had the main verse lick for 'Never Been Sold Before' floating around in my head and it fitted perfectly with Mike's chords. I showed it to Mike and he liked it. We cut that and most of the basics at Sunset Sound in Hollywood.

The opening walking guitar riff is irresistible with Mashbir and Michael Bruce meshing their parts together to give the song a raunchy vibe. Neal and Dennis are clearly well into it too; those typical bubbling Dunaway bass runs are just outstanding. Alice also sounds motivated by this quality material, giving one of his master class lessons in how to put across a lyric. The delivery of, 'I just can't BELIEVE that you're selling me' is a joy to listen to every time. Only Alice can get such mileage out of one word. While we are on the lyrics, Alice pulls off a 'what does he actually mean moment' when he sings, 'I'm sick of streets, chicks and dicks, And I'm, I'm really sick of you'. Of course, he means private detectives when he sings 'dicks', doesn't he?

A minor blemish is that the brass on the instrumental break is over-cooked; there's a really tasty Mashbir guitar solo going on at the time and they should have let him have that moment, turned him way up and killed the brass. Mick: 'The solo was done at the Record Plant NYC. And it was my first 'comped' solo. Three or four passes of improvisation, then Richardson and Douglas compiled the takes into the solo.'

All in all, it's a great song that surprisingly has never been played live.

'Hard Hearted Alice' (Bruce/Cooper)
Mick Mashbir:

'Hard Hearted Alice' was just beginning to form when we worked on it. Mike didn't have music for the chorus and, after some starts and stops the chords just came to me, all at once, like they do sometimes. We were just jammin' some more on it, and we were taking turns playing the rhythm part, and working on some solos, when Mike suggested we trade solos on the record, and that's what we ended up doing. We played them live in the studio together and that's why they came off so well.

Mick adds that he was involved in writing the music with Michael.
It opens gently with Alice's hushed tones, Michael on acoustic and beautiful tinkling bells from Neal. His percussive touches here are

delightful. There is a gear change at the 1:43 mark and things get a lot more lively with Alice putting on the vocal snarl.

Bob Dolin shines on the organ. He is used for the most part to add colour on this album, but here he gets to be a major part of the backing track, even taking a solo at 2:59 during the instrumental break. That break really makes you sit up and take notice. The duelling guitars of Michael Bruce and Mick Mashbir are meshing so well together here, adding grit and fire. Michael comes in with the first guitar solo at 3:07, followed by Mick at 3:17. It then swaps back to Michael at 3:25 before returning to Mick at 3:35. Credit also to the backing rhythm track with great driving percussion from Neal and bass from Dennis. The combination of those two plus Bob and Michael (on rhythm guitar) make for a sinuous wall of sound that is close to Allman Brothers style jamming.

There is another chorus, beautifully sung by Alice, Michael and Bob Dolin, and into a long slow outro ending on a crescendo and the faint shimmer of a gong. It's one of the best songs on the album, and another that deserves to be resurrected for live shows.

'Crazy Little Child' (Bruce/Cooper)

For Neal, this is the worst song the band ever recorded and he says he doesn't even play on the final released version. This is confirmed in Michael's book, and by Allan Schwartzberg, who was the drummer brought in to play the parts. We can assume Alice and Michael both liked the song, as they wrote it. Michael says his original version goes back to his High School days.

There are some nice big-band-style flourishes and Bob Dolin adds a honky-tonk piano part that fits in well. There would have been more flourishes if, according to Schwartzberg, they had used the right take of his drums: 'The drum part that exists today all these years later is NOT the take that was deemed to be the final. I played a New Orleans second line-style drum part that included funky drum rolls throughout'.

Glen might have liked the song and would have added something imaginative to it. Michael agrees: 'If he had been around, Glen would have really been able to come up with something special for that'. Michael Bruce plays all the rhythm guitar, while Mick Mashbir takes the solo at 3:21. It's a sympathetically constructed solo, enhancing the reflective feel of the lyrics. Paul Prestopino adds banjo accompaniment that works better than you might expect.

There is another good section after Mick's solo where Alice sings, 'Questions there were few, facts there were none'. Everything drops down and, backed only by Bob Dolin's piano; he covers the final moments of the 'crazy little child'. This section is masterful and sets things up for the big ending which could have done with being bigger, more drama and panache.

The song has great moments, and Alice does his best to give the lyrics full value and puts in a great performance, but the song itself still comes over as average at best.

'Working Up A Sweat' (Bruce/Cooper)

This side two opener sees Michael pulling another rocker out of his songbook. It's lively and bounces along, but it needed more polish to bring it up to speed. I love some of the little touches like the guitar fills on the verses and Neal's 'fire alarm bells' (1:08). All of the guitars are by Michael, except for the lead guitar fills and solo which are played by Dick Wagner who runs riot as the song goes on. For the harmonica part, they brought in former Canned Heat member Stanley Behrens. Guesting, on the catchy backing vocals are The Pointer Sisters. This is the best use of backing vocals on the album.

The song isn't done any favours by the rather dry production. The dynamics that mark the band's best work were badly needed here.

'Muscle Of Love' (Bruce/Cooper)

Neal: 'My favourite song on that album is "Muscle Of Love"'.

An absolute classic. Imagine this song opening the album and you would have thought business was usual with the band. It comes in with a barnstorming twisting riff that is up there with the best.

That riff, played by Michael, is colossal and his rhythm playing throughout is outstanding, edgy and exciting. Mick Mashbir sits over the top putting in the creamy lead fills and a great solo near the end of the song.

Meanwhile, in the engine room, Dennis and Neal are on top form, especially on the furiously fast ending. It's one of Alice's best vocals too; the way he wraps his voice lasciviously round lines like 'Who's the queen of the locker room, who's the cream of the crop' with delicious emphasis on 'cream'.

In the background on the verses is a curious noise like an engine revving up. It was Dennis who played it live, but it was, he says, executive producer Jack Richardson who got the sound in the studio playing an African squeeze drum.

Adding to the pluses for this track is an absolute beast of an instrumental break that hits you, from 1:29, like a train, heavy and fast. So fast that Michael now admits, 'I wish I could go back and slow the fuck down 'Muscle Of Love'. I wish I had the excuse to say I was on speed. The adrenalin and the bare-knuckles speed of that track is whewwww'.

Mick Mashbir gets in a guitar solo in a style that was quite trendy at that time. 'The solo was played with a talk-box. It was Jack Douglas's idea. One of the studio techs figured out how to make one in about an hour, and that's how that happened'. What's so good about it is how it works so harmoniously with the instrumental backing track, and not out front like Peter Frampton or Joe Walsh's talk-box solos of the era.

This would have been a great single in the UK, except they wouldn't have got the lyrics past the radio stations and BBC. In other, more liberal, parts of the world it was released as an edited single, backed with 'Crazy Little Child'. It didn't chart in America.

'Man With The Golden Gun' (Bruce/Buxton/Cooper/ Dunaway/Smith)

At the end of every James Bond film, the credits used to tell you the title of the next film in the series. The band, all fervent fans, saw this on the credits of *Live And Let Die* and were inspired to write their own tune for the forthcoming *Man With The Golden Gun*. They missed the deadline for the song to be included, which meant that the producers used a terrible song by Lulu.

The song has all the tropes of a classic Bond theme, and the only problem would have been it's a minute too long compared to others that featured in the series. The crisp intro works a treat and sounds exactly like the opening to a Bond theme. Dennis and Neal are well locked in a groove together while Michael and Mick handle the dual rhythm guitars. Dennis's deep notes on the end of each of his phrases give the intro a pulse. Dennis remains, 'very proud of my bass playing on that song'. You can tell that Alice is well up for this track too, performing a Bond song clearly means everything to him.

The instrumental section comes in at 1:19 and the band's enthusiasm for film soundtrack-style music comes to a final glorious zenith here. There's a fat brass section high in the mix while Dolin's throbbing synthesizer is just audible. Also too low in the mix is Liza Minnelli, making her first appearance on the album. Alice is back at 2:07 for another verse and chorus, Liza joining him on the chorus with the backing vocals. It's a missed opportunity, not using her punchy vocals to duet with Alice.

The love of Bond themes sees them going, at 2:37, for a dizzying spiral of chords that are exactly in keeping with the style. The change at 3:05 is the best part of the song – 'But you'll never see him, he'll be looking for you' sings Alice, his voice full of warning. From here it's a surge to the end; Liza, still woefully under-used, does hit the high notes on the final chords as Neal's gong crashes. This is another of the album's high spots.

'Teenage Lament '74' (Cooper/Smith)

Lyrically this is a prequel to 'I'm Eighteen'. Teenage angst at the age of fifteen is on a different level to turning eighteen; it's about trying to keep up with your peers, gold lame jeans and the latest hair-style. Just what are you gonna do?

Despite the angst, it's a musically bright and cheerful song that at 1:38 even recalls the drum pattern from 'Sun Arise' but played slower. The guitar solo, at 2:00, sounds almost like a tribute to Glen and is played by Michael Bruce. It's a great solo, picking up on the frustrated tone of the lyrics. At 2:45 the tempo picks up for a growing Latin workout that hits a peak once the elite names backing chorus takes off at 3:11. Right at the fade, a member of the chorus is chanting 'Alice, Alice, Alice' and it's a shame, as it sounds like they had just found a real groove.

Ironically, one person who wasn't keen on the way the song came out was its main writer. Neal: 'The song I liked least of the ones I had written at the time was 'Teenage Lament' because it had taken such a tangent. It was used as a vehicle for the band you know, mixing with Liza Minnelli and The Pointer Sisters and Ronnie Spector. That was all cool and everything; great publicity.'

It was released as an edited single, backed with 'Hard Hearted Alice', and got to number twelve in the UK and number 48 in America.

'Woman Machine' (Bruce/Buxton/Cooper/Dunaway/Smith)

The song goes back to an early unrecorded Spiders song called 'Mr. Machine'. It's a mystery how it made it on to the album when better songs didn't make the cut. It searches around for any inspiration for the first few minutes, before crashing into life at 2:38 as a great riff comes in. That change of pace and dynamics seems to promise at least a good ending.

It's not to be, the interlude passes and we soon sink back again into the rather average opening stanzas.

A big problem with the song is the tedious chorus which does nothing to lift things. Listening closely on headphones reveals some good guitar parts that would have brightened things up no end if they had been pushed higher in the mix.

Michael plays all the rhythm guitar parts while Mick Mashbir takes lead guitar and the solo, which he is justifiably very proud of. Mick: 'One of my personal favourite solos was on 'Woman Machine'. I was working it up and it just wasn't working for me. Then I saw a Foxx Tone Machine, sitting in a pile of FX pedals, and I tried it out. It worked perfectly and gave the solo that very mechanical sound.'

The final song on the final band album concludes with Alice reading from an Ampex manual. So it was that the band who delivered so much bowed out in the studio.

Related Songs
'Baby Please Don't Stop' (Smith)

This song was rehearsed for the album but didn't make the final cut. A shame as it's a better track than 'Woman Machine' at least, or it could have been worked up for a B-side. Neal sings it, and it might have stayed that way had they recorded it, but it's intriguing to imagine what Alice might have contributed both lyrically and vocally.

The band on this is Neal, Dennis, Michael and Mick Mashbir, with Alice handling the harmonica. The R&B rootsy style plugs right back to the band's early days and it's an enjoyable rough and raw song. Neal finally issued it on his *Platinum God* solo album, a version taken at a slower pace. Apart from Alice, it is the same line-up playing on it, so was presumably recorded at the same sessions.

'Never Been Sold Before – demo' (Bruce/Buxton/Cooper/ Dunaway/Smith)

The demo recording of the song is featured on the *Old School* box-set and is very different with a killer staccato riff and no underlying groove to it. That riff is straight out of Michael's top drawer of classic riffs.

Mick Mashbir didn't recall this version when I sent it to him, but they were right to change things around, because the final recorded track has more polish and class to it. But they should have kept the riff from this version to use elsewhere.

'Respect For The Sleepers' (Bruce/Cooper)

The prototype of the song 'Muscle Of Love'. The title and lyrics are apparently about Glen Buxton, who was known for sleeping in late and liked that to be 'respected'. Musically it's pretty much the same, but the pattern of the lyrics is obviously different due to the change in the subject matter. It's an interesting track, but they were right to come up with new lyrics and give the backing track time to develop more. It is available on the *Life And Crimes* box set.

'Rock 'N' Roll Radio' (Smith)

Neal: 'It was written for *Muscle Of Love,* but it didn't make it on to the album. Luckily it did make it on to the *Battle Axe* album. I would love to have had Alice sing it. It was a tribute to everything as we grew up, and a tribute to the media that made us a hit band'. Michael Bruce also says this song was considered for the album.

The existing demos don't feature it and it's a surprise it wasn't recorded as it would have been terrific with Alice singing it. It was a highlight of Billion Dollar Babies' *Battle Axe* album three years later when Neal sang it.

It should have been one of the definite 'must record' songs for *Muscle Of Love.* It sums up the journey of the group to success via the radio stations and the fans around the world and would have been perfect as the last track on the album. It's a joyous, upbeat celebration of a song that would have made a great single.

'The Lady Is A Tramp' (Lorenz Hart/Richard Rodgers)

Featured as a set piece in the *Good To See You Again* film. It shows our bewigged and suited heroes slumming it as an expensive bar band with an orchestra. Sadly it's not our heroes playing on it, as Michael Bruce explains: 'No that wasn't us, well it was us miming, but the song was recorded by Alice alone'. Alice delivers it with ironic resignation, yet at the same time makes it entertaining listening.

1974: Nothing They Could Say Could Ever Make The Pieces Fit

Alice made his first real solo appearance on 17 January when he filmed 'The Devil Made Me Do It' – an episode of *The Snoop Sisters*. This detective series featured Helen Hayes and Mildred Natwick as two Miss Marple-esque sleuth sisters; Alice appears as 'Prince', and mimes to 'Sick Things'. The *Snoop Sisters* appearance aired in March, as Alice delved further into TV celebrity culture by recording three episodes of the game-show *Hollywood Squares*.

March had been set for a European tour, but it was cancelled before the dates were announced. While the band couldn't maintain their exhausting schedule, if any tour was needed it was surely a European one in order to maintain momentum? Instead, on 28 March, they set off for Sao Paolo and a short five-date tour of Brazil. The set-list was unchanged from The Holiday Tour.

The first night, at Sao Paolo's Anhembi Palacio Das Convencoes, saw them set the world record for indoor attendance at a concert. For Glen, it remained a stand-out memory, as he told *Just Testing* in 1996: 'We played indoors to 150,000 people. You know what that looks like? It's like a field of wheat, but hair! You can't even see the end of the audience'. Mick Mashbir adds: 'The '74 Brazil tour was the band at its live peak. Playing the gig in Sao Paulo was an exceptional experience. We were really peaking as a band when it all ended'. The last night of the tour, on 6 April at Maracanacinho in Rio De Janeiro, was indeed when it all ended, the last time the full Alice Cooper group ever played together.

Cindy reflects on the years on the road:

Travelling all over the world with some of the people I love the most was a gift. It was wonderful being part of such an amazing team, plus I was with the love of my life, Dennis, and my dearly loved brother Neal. London was Dennis's and my favourite city to visit. It was so cool and exciting in the '70s. We usually didn't have much time in each city, but when we had a free day, we'd try and take in the sights and get the feel. Everything was great fun, like one big family, until sadly things started changing.

The illusion that all was still well was kept going with the initial release, in May, of the *Good To See You Again* film that the band had been working on. It was a mix of concert footage from the *Billion Dollar*

Babies tour, plus some set-piece comedy routines. The film was felt to be unsatisfactory and swiftly withdrawn, with a new edit planned for release later in the year.

With the band now on hiatus, the idea of solo albums was discussed. Neal: 'Michael was writing tons of songs and he wanted to take a year off for *In My Own Way* and we all agreed to it. I had *Platinum God* to work on, and that was when Alice went off and did the *Nightmare* album'. In June it was announced in the press that these three were working on solo projects. Bob Dolin and Mick Mashbir helped Michael out, and, on a minor level, Neal too. Neal's main collaborator was, of course, Dennis. Alice, meanwhile, went to the Bahamas with Dick Wagner in July, where they worked on material for what became *Welcome To My Nightmare*. In effect, these solo projects were the beginning of the end for the band.

All five had, and still have, their own perspectives on what went wrong. Glen's opinion has only been publicised once, in that *Just Testing* interview: 'We never ever took time to enjoy the fruits of our labour. All we did was labour. We used to do two albums a year, plus, well, the *Billion Dollar Babies* tour was 90 cities in three months, one day off in 90 days. We just said we gotta take a break and we did, and a couple of the boys worked on some other projects. I was getting interested in videos and things like that. We just drifted apart'. It was different times back then, but if *Muscle Of Love* could have been bumped back to 1974 and the band allowed to make one album per year and tour less, just maybe they could have turned things around. Time also to sort out the issues facing Glen and Alice.

On a happier note, in July Dennis and Cindy got married, making Dennis and Neal brothers-in-law.

In August Alice headed for Toronto, hooking up again with Bob Ezrin, where his nightmare begins. Tiding things over on the record release front that month, and keeping things looking fine for the band, Warners released the *Greatest Hits* album. The newly edited *Good To See You Again* film finally came out in September.

Doubts about the band's future surfaced with the publication in November of Bob Greene's *Billion Dollar Baby* book. This behind the scenes account of the recording of *Muscle Of Love* and the Holiday tour presented a damaging view of inter-band relationships. The band still profess it to be mostly exaggerated nonsense, but in the final analysis you feel that the book must have played a part in the band's demise – if only for exposing the issues around Glen Buxton.

Alice Cooper's Greatest Hits *(Warner Bros.)*

Produced at various studios 1970 to 1973 by Bob Ezrin, Jack Douglas and Jack Richardson
US release date: August 1974. UK release date: August 1974.
Highest chart places: USA: 8, UK: -
Running time: 41:10
Songs:
'I'm Eighteen', 'Is It My Body', 'Desperado', 'Under My Wheels', 'Be My Lover', 'School's Out'
'Hello Hooray', 'Elected', 'No More Mr. Nice Guy', 'Billion Dollar Babies', 'Teenage Lament '74', 'Muscle Of Love'
See the original album credits for musicians, composers and additional musicians

This is easily one of the finest greatest hits albums ever released and perfectly packaged.

Every vinyl and CD release of this album solidly uses the (mostly) longer album versions for all the songs. Other than 'No More Mr Nice Guy' all of the songs on side two were originally issued in edited versions as singles. One glaring omission in the track-list is 'Caught In A Dream', which is replaced by the B-side to 'I'm Eighteen' – 'Is It My Body'. Was that an error?

The two *Love It To Death* tracks were remixed to fit in more stylistically with the remaining tracks. Both are more bassy and have reverb added, particularly noticeable on 'Is It My Body'. Even more noticeable is the addition of an overdriven rhythm guitar part on 'I'm Eighteen'. This part was on the master tapes, but unused on the *Love It To Death* version. Hear it most clearly on the intro where it adds extra heaviness to the sound.

At this point, it's worth noting that none of these singles featured a non-album B-side. The only 'spare' tracks they had ('Nobody Likes Me' and 'Slick Black Limousine') both ended up on flexi-disc give-aways. Dennis:

Record companies wanted the B-side to be a song that had little chance of getting radio play because they wanted all of the stations to play the same song so it could have a better shot at becoming a hit. We had some say, but the record company experts, with some input from the producer, had the final say on the singles.

The cover is a work of art. Designer Ernie Cefalu was immediately enthused by the title. 'For me the greatest hits in America is the Saint Valentine's Day Massacre from that gangster era, so let's have the band with the violin cases sitting on the car on the cover, and then when you go inside it's a dance marathon, which were really big in that era'.

Drew Struzan did the outer sleeve illustration showing our heroes with an array of Hollywood stars of the era in attendance. There are subtle nods in the design to the tracks on the album too – the garage address is '18' and the newspapers read 'School's Out' etc. The inside sleeve drawing of the dance marathon was by Bill Garland.

Brilliant as it is, the cover ran into problems when it was submitted. Ernie:

We went to Warner Brothers to turn the designs in and they rejected them because we had people portrayed on the inside and the outside that were still alive. So we had to change those people out. For example, Mickey Rooney was dancing with Judy Garland on the inside. He was still alive, but we just couldn't put ANY movie star's face on the body – they had to be pretty much physically the same. We found Alan Ladd was a short guy, so we put him in there dancing with Judy Garland.

As a summary of the peak they were at with that glorious run of singles, the cover designs sum it all up perfectly.

1975: Up And Down Alone

The first clue to the band splitting came when Alice appeared on *The Smothers Brothers Show* on 11 January performing 'Unfinished Sweet' on his own. But the more far-reaching development was Alice signing his own deal for a solo album, upsetting Warners as it wasn't with them. It was claimed that this was to be the soundtrack album to a TV special – and thus exempt from the terms of the Warners contract. It allowed Shep and Alice to seek a better deal for this one-off project and in the end, they went with Atlantic in the U.S.A. and Anchor in the UK. *Welcome To My Nightmare* was released on 4 March, coming out before Alice had even recorded the TV special it was supposed to be the soundtrack for!

It was time to tour the album, and backing him were the core band from the sessions – Dick Wagner and Steve Hunter (guitars), Prakash John (bass), Jozef Chirowkski (keyboards) and Pentti Glan (drums). All but Chirowski had last been out together as Lou Reed's band, and the two axe heroes had already appeared on previous Cooper albums. All were supremely talented musicians, but it would be nigh on impossible to match the old band's charisma. Any contrasts were neatly avoided by putting Alice firmly out in front as the star of the show, apart from the guitar duel sequence for Wagner and Hunter.

Prakash John hadn't been sure about the tour: 'They asked me to do it, and I thought I'm getting deeper into this, but I'm so glad I didn't say, 'You know what, I'd rather not do it'. I had turned down chances in the past, such as when Bobby Whitlock invited me to play bass in Derek and the Dominoes and I said no'. Johnny Badanjek was originally considered as the drummer for the tour: 'Bob (Ezrin) asked what my plans were about going on the road. I had other commitments at the time and couldn't do it'. Also in the stage party were the dancers, including Sheryl Goddard, who was soon to become a very big part of Alice's life.

Alice's live debut as a solo artist came at the Wings Stadium in Kalamazoo, Michigan on 21 March. Steve Hunter told Jeb Wright of *Classic Rock Revisited* that:

It was packed, and I remember when I came out to go on stage and I saw that many people, I was completely blown away. At that moment, I knew it was going to be a fun ride. They were accepting Alice as a solo artist. Part of that was because the album was strong.

The set-list focussed on the new album: 'Welcome To My Nightmare', 'Years Ago', 'No More Mr. Nice Guy', 'Years Ago', 'Billion Dollar Babies', 'Years Ago', 'I'm Eighteen', 'Years Ago', 'Some Folks', 'Cold Ethyl', 'Only Women Bleed', 'Devil's Food', 'The Guitar Jam', 'The Black Widow', 'Steven', 'Welcome To My Nightmare (reprise)', 'Escape', 'Escape (reprise)'/'School's Out', 'Department Of Youth'.

Only 'The Awakening' was missing, a surprise given its brevity. The use of 'Years Ago' to link to the older songs was clever. Prakash John, for one, was happy to play the classics, especially 'School's Out'. 'I really liked playing that because it's basically a blues minor-key shuffle. I got to wind out a bit on that tune and Alice would give me a solo because it was the encore'.

Alice was surprised once by a variation that occurred in the set. Prakash: 'In 'Steven', we were playing that bit where it goes 'Steeveennn' and Alice makes a few responses, so Joey (Chirowski) starts to insert a bit of 'Popeye The Sailor Man'. Alice was in stitches. There's 15,000 people in front of us and we were just killing ourselves. You can sometimes take those liberties. Alice was right into it, so it wasn't something done to challenge his authority.'

On 29 March they played at Erie County Fieldhouse in Pennsylvania. Prakash John remembers the date and his friend Jozef Chirowski. 'Joey was always a bit of a different guy. A lovely person, happy and jovial, but deep down inside a lot of these guys who are comedians have a silent dark side. By that, I mean loneliness. I introduced him to this girl at a show in Eyrie and he married her'. The spirit among the band was very strong with great camaraderie. Prakash recalls that 'Joey, Wagner and Whitey Glan would keep our limo in stitches. People used to fight to get into that limo. Wagner was a hilarious, witty person, funny as hell'.

Alice's new single was released in April. 'Only Women' had the 'bleed' dropped from the title there, and also in the UK, in an effort to reduce any reluctance to play-list it.

If you couldn't see the tour itself, there was a bonus at the end of April when *The Nightmare* TV special aired on ABC, while the second night at the Los Angeles Forum, on 19 June, was recorded for the *King Biscuit Hour* show.

Each night there proved to be an unexpected bonus for Alice on stage. The sequence from 'Cold Ethyl' through to 'Only Women Bleed 'had become one that he looked forward to every night, as he got to be up close and personal with Sheryl Goddard. Their romance blossomed on-stage and off. Alice was a free agent having split with his long-time girlfriend Cindy (Cynthia) Lang.

The future of the tour was put in doubt on 23 June when Alice fell off the stage at the Pacific Coliseum, Vancouver. Prakash: 'We just had to keep playing. There's a certain skill to playing in a rock rhythm section; you are not as tied in as you are in a rhythm and blues setting which is cosy and tight'. In spite of breaking six ribs and being concussed, Alice eventually returned to the stage, managing to perform a few more songs before having to stop. The pressures of keeping from cancelling dates meant that he only got the three-day gap before Edmonton, Alberta to recuperate. It was decided to go ahead with that show and Alice lasted 35 minutes before having to stop with breathing difficulties. Incredibly, after two further days off, the tour picked up again without further issues.

'Department Of Youth', was released as a single in July. While it was still a hoped-for hit, Alice turned up at New York's Riverside Park on 12 August in a clean up the park promotion. Supporting him were the department of youth, in the guise of a few hundred children.

At some point in 1975, Michael Bruce's solo album was released. *In My Own Way* came out on Polydor in Germany and showcased Michael's abilities as a singer/songwriter. Alice puts in an appearance guesting on the song 'As Rock Rolls On' and there are two strong covers in the form of The Easybeats' 'Friday On My Mind' and Slade's' So Far So Good'. It's a good album and it would have been nice to see more releases from Michael. The missing solo album was Neal Smith's *Platinum God*, which finally emerged in 1999. Like Michael, he deserved far more attention and plaudits, and his album should have had record companies queuing to release it.

Warners were keen for the contract they held to be fulfilled by Alice and in August they demanded an album be delivered to them. But before recordings were possible, Alice had a European tour to fulfil. He flew into London on 9 September for an interview on the Russell Harty TV show, promoting three British gigs – two at Wembley Empire Pool and one at the Liverpool Empire. One of the Wembley shows was late starting because of visitors to see Alice. Prakash:

Peter Sellers was there with Ringo Starr in our dressing room before the show. He had us laughing, killing ourselves. He saw me and talked to me in that Bombay English which he used to be excellent at. We had to hold up the show for twenty minutes because we had to gain our composure.

After gigs in Germany Alice flew back to New York for a rest before forthcoming dates in Australia and New Zealand. In the meantime,

'Welcome To My Nightmare' was released as a single in October. However, the tour down under, set for November, was cancelled. There had been issues with the Australian Immigration Department, saying Alice was banned for his degenerate influence. They had lifted the ban by September, but the cancellation of the tour came anyway. In hindsight, it looked like a much-needed break.

Dates were still to come in America, where a week-long residency was booked in December at the High Sierra Theater, Lake Tahoe. The band was the same, other than Danny Weiss (of Iron Butterfly) deputising for an indisposed Steve Hunter. A welcome surprise on the opening night was Vincent Price walking on to deliver his macabre monologue.

Alice had done it. A successful album and tour gave him options to pursue a solo career. But sadly it also meant there would be no reunion with the original band for many years.

Welcome To My Nightmare (Atlantic/Anchor)

Personnel:

Alice Cooper: vocals

Dick Wagner: electric and acoustic guitar, vocals

Steve Hunter: electric guitar

Bob Ezrin: keyboards, piano, synthesiser, harmonium

Jozef Chirowski: keyboards, clavinet, Fender Rhodes, harpsichord

Prakash John: bass

Pentti Glan: drums

with:

Johnny 'Bee' Badanjek: drums on 'Welcome To My Nightmare', 'The Black Widow' and 'Escape'

Tony Levin: bass on 'Welcome To My Nightmare' and 'Escape'

Trish McKinnon: vocals on 'Steven'

Vincent Price: curator

and:

David Ezrin, Gerry Lyons, Michael Sherman and The Summerhill Children's Choir: backing vocals

Produced at Soundstage, Toronto; The Record Plant, New York; Electric Lady, New York; A&R Studios, New York, 1974-1975 by Bob Ezrin.

USA release date: 11 March 1975. UK release date: 15 March 1975

Highest chart places: USA: 5, UK: 19

Running time: 43:19

Any time I'm gonna work on a theatrically based album, the first thing
that comes to mind is Bob Ezrin. I mean, look at the track record we had.
Alice Cooper: *Making Of Welcome To My Nightmare* video

As a purchaser back in 1975 it was not apparent to me, or other fans I
knew, that Alice was going to stay as a solo performer and that this was
the end for the original band. The hope I, and many others, had was that
it was an interlude or diversion. Something to savour while waiting for
the next band album. The message that this was Alice Cooper 'solo', not
band, comes across strongly on the front cover. There *he* is welcoming us
to *his* nightmare. Alice alone. The cover was illustrated and designed by
Drew Struzan. Ernie Cefalu:

Drew spent the day doing a beautiful pencil drawing of Alice. The next
day I came into the office and he'd put a brown sepia tone wash over the
whole thing. I freaked out and said, 'What did you do, what happened?'
He said, 'Don't worry, that's how I work. The middle tone is the base
and then I work darker and lighter, always keeping that middle tone. So
if you look at that cover, you will see little pieces of the sepia tone here
and there. He painted over and started at the top left and finished at the
bottom right in oil. It was like working with Michelangelo or Leonardo Da
Vinci – the guy was that good.

It's a great cover, but it perhaps needed more of a sense of menace in the
vein of the later *Last Temptation* cover, although the background insect
drawings have an unsettling feel.

Alice, Shep Gordon and Bob Ezrin had always planned for this to be
a project working across three areas – concept album, stage show and
film. Ezrin told James Campion (for his book *Shout It Out Loud*) that
the original story was to have been about a rock star named Steven who
survives a plane crash in an icy mountain range. With this idea in mind,
he and Alice went to meet their prospective director. Bob Ezrin (from the
making of the album video):

Danny Mann, the director who was going to direct this picture, was
shooting a film with Vincent Price and Donald Pleasance (*Journey Into
Fear*). We went on board ship with them in Vancouver and Vincent Price
was there, smoking a cigar. I looked at this big tall guy and I listened to his
voice and I said: 'How would you like to make your rock 'n' roll debut?'

The plot was abandoned and replaced by the story of Steven – a boy in bed with his nightmares. But some of the music from the original story was used in the eventual album, as was Vincent Price. The big challenge for Alice and Ezrin was how to cover the loss of the diverse input from the old band. It's something they partly manage, but what they ultimately come up with is a different and glossier take on the Alice Cooper form.

Dick Wagner came on board as Alice's main songwriting partner, and also took the guitar parts with his old buddy Steve Hunter. Alice told *Guitar World's* Brad Tolinkski in 2018: 'Both were spectacular lead players. Steve might've been the better soloist, but Dick was the better writer'. Both had been credited before on the Cooper Group albums but not explicitly, other than Dick's part on 'My Stars'. Now it was time for them to shine with full credit. The rhythm guitar parts were played by both men, a practice they would continue each time they played together. Steve explains that for the lead parts, 'Dick and I sat down and went over each thing song-by-song and decided between us who would play what solo where, so it came out even. It was important to both of us that we did that'.

Pentti Glan played most of the drums, with Johnny Badanjek also involved. 'Bob Ezrin asked me to come up from Detroit and play drums on a few tracks that he had in mind for my style of playing'. One of the studio visitors made an impression on Johnny:

Alice had a female friend whose son he let come to the studio every day and hang out. He was around eight or nine years old and was my pinball partner. I asked him one day what his name was and he said, 'Keanu'! I said, 'That's a pretty cool name'. He said, 'It's Hawaiian'. He was very nice, and it was good to see him become a great actor and do good.

Pentti's rhythm section partner of many years, Prakash John, took on most of the bass duties. He welcomed the care that was taken to make him feel involved.

I am grateful to Wagner, Bob and Alice, for explaining the songs and the purpose when we were recording, rather than just hammering them out. I liked the concept of what they were producing. It was unlike most of the other rock I had heard. It was interesting because the chord changes and the songs were being initially sung by Wagner, who wrote most of them. I enjoyed playing with Wagner and Hunter, tremendous devastating rock guitar players and they were very lyrical in their playing.

The album also marks the 'Alice' debut of Tony Levin on bass, Jozef Chirowski on keyboards and Michael Sherman on backing vocals. Sherman was a Toronto based singer who had had success on the folk scene there in the mid to late-sixties.

The 5.1 audio release of the album included an interview with Bob Ezrin and Alice Cooper about the making of the album. Their quotes here are taken from that interview unless otherwise stated.

'Welcome To My Nightmare' (Cooper/Wagner)

Alice: 'That bass line set up the whole overture'.

An atmospheric opening without the drama we usually associate with a Cooper opening cut. Alice welcomes us and eases us in. It looks different, yes, but in the end, 'I think you're gonna like it'. There is an attractive instrumental bridge at 1:54 that is pure film soundtrack-inspired and then, at 2:28, the second half of the song kicks in. Badanjek plays a great fill at 3:01 and cues in an increasingly urgent and demonstrative Alice, the quiet lure of the opening phrases now gone. The brass turns up the heat and Badanjek's drumming gives the music the power it needs.

The solo that comes in after the breakdown explosion is Jozef Chirowski going wild on the clavinet with a wah-wah pedal. Frustratingly the song fades out slowly when surely a big dramatic flourish was called for.

It was the third (edited) single off the album. In Britain, it was backed with 'The Black Widow' and didn't trouble the charts. It got to number 45 in America, where it was backed with 'Cold Ethyl'.

'Devil's Food' (Cooper/Ezrin/Kelly Jay)

A stinging opening riff from Wagner, which this brief song then hangs on to. Phased effects on the guitars and a steady heavy rock vibe dominate until the slow fade out. At 1:45 we effectively segue into a different track where we meet the curator for a guided tour of the Arachnida collection. Vincent Price gives an enthralling monologue as the Curator. His delivery and emphasis is a joy, with every word given the right measure. His performance obviously thrilled Michael Jackson!

The track is frustrating because the 1:45 of song we do get could have been developed into a longer piece. The Curator section, which runs from 1:45 to the track's end at 3:35, would have been better given credit as a separate track, and at one time that was the intention. Price's monologue was to be known as 'Jolly Macabre: Tour Guide at the Pasadena Palace of Insects'. Alice:

He was like a little kid in the studio. He came in and he goes, 'Would I be able to change some of this?' I said, 'You're Vincent Price! You can do anything you want'. He changed a few lines and played with it a little bit here and there. And he would get in the middle of something and say it and he would start giggling because he liked it so much.

Co-writer of the first half of the track Kelly Jay (aka Henry Fordham), was a member of the Canadian band Crowbar, who also featured Jozef Chirowski.

'The Black Widow' (Cooper/Wagner/Ezrin)
The Cooper/Ezrin/Wagner axis were sparking off each other, the muse coming fast. Ezrin:

He (Alice) was in a corner of the studio writing away and he goes, 'Wait wait what about this?' And he goes: 'The horror of his sting, the horror that he brings, the unholiest of kings The Black Widow'. And Wagner goes da da da da da da dah. The song is there, we're off to the races!

This is the heaviest track on the album, but while Alice gives the vocal his all, there is something unsatisfying about the music, which in the first two and a half minutes is stodgy. Wagner's guitar solo doesn't get out of the aural soup, just adding to it. There are no real dynamics until 2:35 when at last the sound opens up with Johnny Badanjek's drums leading into an interestingly different soundscape. This last-minute or so of the song has more room to breathe and is all the better for it, even with the brass section added to the mix.

'Some Folks' (Cooper/Alan Gordon/Ezrin)
A reference point for the song was Peggy Lee's 'Fever', and it was obviously set up as a showpiece tune for the live set. Prakash: 'For me to play this it helped to know the personality of the song, and understand what the show was going to be like'.

On record, this finger-clicking Broadway tune came as a surprise. There had always been Broadway influences, but this was by far the most overt example yet. It's an engaging song, with a conspiratorial vocal tone from Alice and a lively backing track that hits all the right spots.

The brass touches throughout are a particular delight, adding emphasis when needed. The faster section from 2:02 has some clever Morse code-like guitar touches in the background as Steve Hunter takes off on a solo. He gets more ferocious solos after that, particularly from 3:35 onwards when the band steps up several gears. The outro is delightful with a final razzmatazz flourish.

'Only Women Bleed' (Cooper/Wagner)

Amongst the demos Dick Wagner played Alice was a song he had written for his band The Frost in 1968. The Frost never recorded 'Keep Movin' On' and Dick didn't expect Alice to be enthusiastic given it was a ballad. To his surprise, Alice liked it – well, the music anyway. Inspired by the tune, Alice put pen to paper and under an hour later had the lyrics for this Cooper classic. This was a different song for him, a move into new areas. Prakash John was impressed:

> The piece that gave me the biggest challenge and emotional connection was 'Only Women Bleed'. Recording it right on the studio floor at Nimbus 9 in Toronto with the entire Toronto Symphony on the floor with us. I used to be a violinist when I was a child in India, so this was a big thrill for me. The bridge is just fantastic. I really thought it was a soulful song, and Alice did a terrific job of delivering it. You know, you don't think of Alice as a classic singer, and I am not playing him down for that, but when he sang that tune, it gave me the chills.

There was some difficulty getting this song down as Bob Ezrin explained:

> We were on our second or third day, trying to get the arrangement right. I had my secretary go and book a little mini circus to arrive that afternoon and come through the studio. So we're working on this heavy song and people are just dragging their asses. All of a sudden the doors open up and whistles blow and tambourines beat and bells are rung and in comes the circus, literally. There's clowns, there's midgets, there's jugglers, there's guys on unicycles and they come in to the studio and start performing and the band is like, 'What is going on'. Then the great thing was the band immediately broke into (circus music) for the circus, and the circus was playing for the band and it was just a wonderful moment. It lasted no more than ten minutes and as quickly as they blew in, they blew out. The doors closed and I said, 'Right, roll 'em', and that was the take on 'Only Women Bleed'.

The instrumental break, from 2:19, is one of the parts salvaged from the original 'rock-star in mountains plane crash' story. This part was written to go with the section of the story when they are digging him out of the snow after an avalanche. That section also crops up again in 'The Awakening'.

The arrangement for the Toronto Symphony Orchestra is superb, but several of the musicians didn't take well to being told what to do by Ezrin. All of that ceased when Ezrin stopped a take to say that a string on one of the cellos was slightly flat. To the musicians' collective amazement, this turned out to be so. Respect was now duly given, and the session proceeded smoothly. Also astounded was Alice, whose reaction was quoted in the *New York Times* in 2005, 'I told Bob, 'That's really amazing, that you could hear that', and he goes, 'I didn't hear anything! When they took their coffee break, I made sure his string was flat.''

Prakash John took the opportunity of the orchestra session to get a part in:

> On the intro, there's a little guitar thing and I do this little slide on the bass. Ezrin told me no, don't do that. But in my head, I thought that's the perfect thing for the intro. So, I waited until the whole Symphony was there on the floor, and it was really cheeky and gutsy of me to do it, and I did that part and it's on the record and it's like a hook at the start. God knows why Bob didn't want me to play it, but he let it go.

The success of this song, particularly as a single, paved the way for a ballad on subsequent albums. A heavily edited version was released as the second single. It was backed with 'Devil's Food' in Britain and didn't chart, but in America, it got to number twelve, backed with 'Cold Ethyl'.

'Department Of Youth' (Cooper/Wagner/Ezrin)

> 'Department of Youth' was the second song I wrote with Alice.
> **Dick Wagner to *Legendary Rock* in 2012**

Prakash John recognised that the song was essentially, 'another "School's Out". An anthemic song that was in keeping with the age group that supported him'. Alice tips his top hat to the 'glam' classic singles of his past, the song fitting in quite easily alongside that run of hits. It's a hugely enjoyable song which has nothing to do with the nightmare theme – perhaps we needed a half-time break!

Pentti Glan's drums are huge and the groove with Prakash John is tremendous, while Chirowski's organ work makes the sound thicker without it being a swamp. Wagner and Hunter get some great riffs in too that chatter and grind around the bass and drum pulse. The final pay-off on the outro of Donny Osmond being the one who gave us 'the power', and not Alice, is a lovely touch.

One of the backing vocalists is Bob Ezrin's then nine-year-old son David. David also appeared on Kiss's 'God Of Thunder', on their *Destroyer* album, playing in the background with his brother Josh.

It's a song Neal Smith liked, 'It was a real Alice Cooper Group song'. Michael agrees with him, 'Yes it's a 'You Drive Me Nervous' or 'Under My Wheels' type song'. Neal adds that apart from this one song, 'The album had lost what the band had'.

An obvious choice for the first single but it didn't do as well as it deserved to. This edited version didn't chart in Britain (backed with 'Cold Ethyl'), and it only reached number 67 in America (backed with 'Some Folks').

'Cold Ethyl' (Cooper/Ezrin)

Back to the freezer after the earlier exploits of 'Refrigerator Heaven'. It's got much more unsavoury since then with the occupant of the fridge. Now we are getting very down and dirty – Steve Hunter's guitar squealing excitedly over some raunchy fuzzy rhythm from Dick Wagner. We are still firmly in rock territory and side two, so far, has a much more orthodox feel to it. Worryingly Ethyl seems to come back to life at times, 1:37 for example, and the only female performer on the album, Trish McKinnon, is 'playing' his mother! Could this be her here too?

The band are having a real ball playing this track, and it's one of the best things on the album. Some of the grit and dirt that had otherwise been smoothed over remains here.

'Years Ago' (Cooper/Wagner)

Dick Wagner (to *Legendary Rock* in 2012): 'That song was started with a little piece of music I had written. He comes out of the toy-box and starts talking about his past and experiences and is already IN the nightmare. Hence the title 'Years Ago', he's talking about his past.'

It's set in a fairground, and not the kind you would want to spend any time in. The rise and fall in the guitar melody line captures the carousel experience perfectly, made explicit in the 'Nightmare' TV special. Chirowski's keyboards, and what sounds like an accordion, build up the fairground feel. At the heart of it all, the counter-play between the two Alice voices – the child and the adult – is disturbing.

Mom is 'played' by Trish McKinnon, better known as the folk singer Patrician-Anne. She does very little, just calling for Steven to come home, but it's memorable. Something in the haunting way she delivers the lines stays with you forever. It's the first time that the boy's name is mentioned on the album.

The voices you hear talking excitedly in the background were said, by Alice, to be from a recording of an exorcism.

'Steven' (Cooper/Ezrin)

A masterpiece. A Mozart-like classical piano part opens the song, with hard plucked strings coming in for contrast. The song 'I Wanna Go To Marz' by John Grant owes a big debt to that piano part.

Alice delivers the verses in the cracking fragile tones of a young boy on the edge of despair. When he gets to 'I don't like to hear you cry, you just don't know how deep that cuts me', it almost feels too intrusive to keep listening. At 1:29 the first of the big choruses comes in, Alice's vocals given extra power with the backing vocalists, while the music keeps crashing round and round. The instrumental bridge at 2:08 is a full band and orchestral version of the opening theme and chorus melody. It dies back to the piano again at 2:43 before rising back up for Dick Wagner's solo at 3:13 which closely follows the melody line.

The 'death scene' that follows leads to the eerie whispered wake up calls at 4:19. As he slowly wakes, Steven loses the voice of the little boy, growing in strength. Steve Hunter's guitar bursts out of the wall of sound with beautifully constructed wailing notes.

A slight pause to catch your breath, there's something evil lurking ahead in the silence.

'The Awakening' (Cooper/Wagner/Ezrin)

Part of the melody, from 0:33 onwards, is also used in 'Only Women Bleed' (from 2:19 onwards), which makes for an interesting link. Alice uses his sinister voice (as per 'Dwight Fry') to set the scene. The eerie quietness of the song, with those alarming dripping noises, gives way to real horror when he sings, 'These crimson spots are dripping from my hands'. It slowly fades out and with it the end of the nightmare itself.

This track is a good example of how Pentti Glan seems to do little but does it effectively with delicate touches as well as the funereal dead drum beats. Prakash: 'He would play some of the most beautiful handwork. He could play all kinds of interesting things– a unique player. You listen to some of the stuff he's playing and it's magical'.

'Escape' (Cooper/Kim Fowley/Mark Anthony)

Nightmare over, a grateful Alice escapes for this closing track, which is another in the tradition of his previous work with the Cooper Group. It's a riff-driven song with cowbell percussion, simple and infectious. The bridge section at 1:12, 'But where am I running to, there's no place to go', is an effective switch to a poppier '60s vibe, before crashing back into the riff-laden verses and choruses. There are some lovely touches on what sounds like a xylophone coming through high in the mix as we head for the outro, and some final great soloing by Wagner.

The original version was recorded by The Hollywood Stars. The riff and the chorus are instantly recognisable and it's worth a listen to hear what Alice did to the song when he took it on. Dick Wagner says in his book that he also contributed to the re-writing of 'Escape', but was uncredited.

Bob Ezrin clearly had a lot of time for The Hollywood Stars as he also picked up their 'King Of The Night Time World' for Kiss's *Destroyer.*

Related Songs
'I'm Flash' (Steve Hammond/Dave Pierce/Bonnie Pierce)

The first track from the multiple artist *Flash Fearless* 'concept' album is pretty good. A lot of that has to do with Alice himself who gives a full-on bravura vocal performance putting real life and energy into the song. It's astonishing, however, just how average the backing band sound on this. The rhythm section is John Entwistle and Bill Bruford!

'Space Pirates' (Steve Hammond/Dave Pierce)

Alice has a hard time getting any mileage out of this turgid song, his second track on 'Flash Fearless'. The backing band features Entwistle again, joined by future bandmate Kenney Jones on drums, Justin Hayward on guitars and Nicky Hopkins on piano. Oh, Keith Moon also turns up as Long John Silver.

Archive releases
Live At The L.A. Forum 1975 (CD)

A stunning quality radio recording. It's the complete show and is available under numerous names on numerous labels. It was a great night for

Alice and the band, and even without the striking visuals, it comes over well. The live set-up gives the *Nightmare* album tracks a different feel. A highlight of the set is the 12:54 medley 'Devil's Food'/'Black Widow' featuring the extended guitar battle between Hunter and Wagner. Prakash: 'It was very entertaining and both those guys were electrifying. But sometimes I wondered if they were competing with each other'.

The Nightmare (DVD)
The film that the album was intended to be the soundtrack to, stands up well, both visually and musically. It's around 25 minutes longer than the album, which makes for a more immersive experience, but the bulk of that extra time is a lot more content from Vincent Price (sometimes with Alice speaking as well).

The lyrics to the *Nightmare* songs are different in places because they had to be made 'appropriate' for television viewing. There are also one or two different guitar parts used. The songs are more or less the same length, apart from 'Some Folks', which is a full minute longer with an extended intro of Pentti Glan's hot cymbal strokes and finger clicks.

A surprise inclusion is 'Ballad Of Dwight Fry', which features the original music by the old band, with a new Alice vocal. While he performs it well, it is curiously out of place.

The versions of 'Devil's Food', 'Cold Ethyl' and 'The Awakening' made it on to the reissued original album as bonus tracks.

Welcome To My Nightmare (DVD)
The two concerts at The Empire Pool, Wembley in 1975 were edited to provide this film. It's a complete run-through and gives you the full impact of the show – giant Cyclops, spiders and all! Film quality is a little grainy, but it's good enough, making for an essential item for your collection.

Welcome To My Nightmare (DVD audio)
Bob Ezrin oversaw the mix of the album for 5.1 surround sound. Apart from balancing the mix for five channels, he also featured elements that had not been in the original stereo mix. Most notable is the inclusion of some of the different lyrics for 'Devil's Food' and more guitar featured on 'Cold Ethyl'.

1976: Could We Discuss My Grave Situation

On 20 March Alice married Sheryl Goddard. The happy couple tied the knot in Acapulco and then were joined by Dick Wagner (and his wife) to write the next album. Songwriting completed, the new album was recorded in Toronto, New York and Los Angeles.

Alice Cooper Goes To Hell was released on 29 June, preceded by a single of 'I Never Cry'. On top of these two releases, his *Me Alice* autobiography was published.

Twenty-five dates were confirmed for the first leg of touring to promote the album, kicking off on 30 June in Halifax, Nova Scotia. But disaster struck, Alice collapsed just before the rehearsals had been due to start and was diagnosed with anaemia. Instead of touring, he went to Barbados for two weeks of sun, relaxation, and probably golf. On his return, alternative plans were put together to promote the album via television appearances.

He was back on form with a bang, many of them in fact, for the Rock Music Awards Show on 19 September, which he co-hosted with Diana Ross. Alice played up to his rebellious image throughout the show and ended up storming off amidst security interventions and explosions, culminating in him pulling a member of the audience, Sheryl, out of her seat. Dancers appeared for a routine to 'Go To Hell' which cut before Alice's solo lead vocal and segued into 'Wish You Were Here'.

The quietest year of his career so far finished with more recording sessions. In December he joined up with Bob Ezrin and the team in Toronto to record a new album for Warners. He had a new character in mind to explore.

Alice Cooper Goes To Hell (Warner Bros.)

Personnel:
Alice Cooper: vocals
Dick Wagner: electric and acoustic guitar, vocals
Steve Hunter: electric guitar
John Tropea: guitars on all tracks except 'Going Home', arrangements.
Bob Ezrin: keyboards, piano, synthesiser, arrangements
Tony Levin: bass
Allan Schwartzberg: drums
Jimmy Maelen: percussion
with:
Bob Babbitt: bass on 'Go To Hell'

Dick Berg: french horn on 'I Never Cry'
Jim Gordon: drums on 'I'm The Coolest', 'I'm Always Chasing Rainbows' and 'Going Home'
Al MacMillan: arrangements
and:
Joe Gannon, Shep Gordon, Shawne Jackson, Bill Misener, Colina Phillips, Michael Sherman, Denny Vosburgh, Laurel Ward, Sharon Lee Williams: backing vocals
Produced at Soundstage, Toronto; The Record Plant, New York; Electric Lady, New York; RCA Studios Los Angeles, 1976 by Bob Ezrin.
USA release date: 25 June 1976. UK release date: 24 July 1976
Highest chart places: USA: 27, UK: 23
Running time: 43:15

Conceptually this album is loosely linked to *Nightmare*, being described in the inner sleeve as a bedtime story for Steven.

There is something familiar about the close-up of Alice's smiling green-tinted face on the front cover. The reason being that his 'head' is taken and cropped from the group picture on the inside sleeve of *Billion Dollar Babies*. The back cover shot of him walking down the steps to hell is equally uninspiring and is also a cut and pasted picture of an older Alice. The lack of new images, one suspects, was prompted by circumstances.

Musically it was decided to make some changes and, to this end, three key musicians were added to the mix. These being John Tropea (guitars), Allan Schwartzberg (drums) and Jimmy Maelen (percussion). Schwartzberg: 'Myself, John Tropea and Jimmy all had roots in jazz and R'n'B. Tony Levin was pure jazz too. So yeah it was like a different movie. You're seeing another side and pretty sophisticated too'. John Tropea concurs: 'I wasn't so familiar with Alice Cooper. I thought he was great and it was a nice turn for him to do these types of songs.'

In the album credits Tropea's contributions are listed on five songs with an additional credit for arrangements. In reality, this is not the case as his guitar work can be heard on every track except for 'Going Home', and he helped with the arrangements on that! On several songs, his guitar is doubled with Hunter (or Wagner) to add an extra dimension to the sound. He recalled how he got the gig, and the set-up at the Record Plant:

I surmised I got on the record because Ezrin liked the first big album I put out called *Tropea*. I was booked for a week at the Record Plant. I did tracks from Monday to Thursday with the rest of the guys. On the

Friday, Jimmy Maelen came in with me and we did overdubs on the whole record. I was impressed with Ezrin, how he put the arrangements and songs together. He was a very creative and talented man. He was very good at telling everybody what to play. He would sit down at the piano and say, I want you to start with this John, this approach. Or he might say to Steve – see what John's playing over there. Let's double it and try and get a better sound on it. I respected him very much and I liked Ezrin a lot.

Allan Schwartzberg rates Ezrin as the best producer he's worked with:

He's one of those guys that could diagnose a record and know where to fix it. There was a point in the sessions where he went around the room and picked up everybody's instrument, and he would play a part and say, 'What do you think of maybe trying something like this', and he played cool stuff for us, he really did. Then he sang the reference vocal. Then in the same session the engineer got sick and had to go home, Bob kept the reference vocal and engineered the rest of the date. He just knows how to do that stuff; he was born to do it. He knows all the instruments. Bob Ezrin is just absolutely dazzling, brilliant in the studio.

As well as coming back for the overdubs Jimmy Maelen was also there for the tracking sessions. Schwartzberg: 'I would try to get Jimmy on every single thing I could, and vice versa. I would always push for Jimmy playing live with me. We worked well together and he was my best friend. It was just great to lock in with somebody like him, who had great time'.

The musicians are credited collectively as The Hollywood Vampires, a reference to Alice's old drinking club. He would resurrect that name years later. Returning for the album were Wagner, Hunter and Tony Levin. Steve Hunter prefers it to *Lace And Whiskey,* although he says, 'We were actually recording both albums at the same time, so it all became a blur'. Which of the additional tracks recorded were saved for *Lace And Whiskey* is open to conjecture.

Along with the returning Michael Sherman, the backing vocalists featured other amazing talent. Bill Misener (aka Bill Marion) had been lead singer/guitarist with Canadian band The Paupers, before going on to sing back-ups on a host of albums. Colina Phillips sang on the Toronto music scene from her teens. In 1985 she recorded the theme to the musical *Yuppies* with Shawne Jackson and Sharon Lee-Williams. Jackson sang with Toronto based band The Majestics, while Lee-Williams sang back-ups for many artists. If you ever watched *Fraggle Rock,* you will have heard Sharon Lee-Williams as she not only sang in it, she also did some of the character voices. Laurel Black (nee Ward) started off singing in musicals, notably *Hair.* Her biggest successes came when she recorded with her future husband Terry Black as Black and Ward. The remaining three backing vocalists include Shep Gordon, Denny Vosburgh (part of the management team), and stage designer Joe Gannon.

The album's step towards a more mainstream Alice is reflected in the more accessible nature of the songs, polished with a typical Ezrin production. Listening again to the album after many years Allan Schwartzberg marvels at it. 'I was so knocked out with the productions. They are just cinematic and theatre-like, and Alice is acting/singing so well. His ability to put a song over is terrific and the guitars are spectacular'.

'Go To Hell' (Cooper/Wagner/Ezrin)

The opening track sets a delicious mood. The intro bass by Motown 'Funk Brother' Bob Babbitt is a pulsing slow groove, with great percussion from Jimmy Maelen. John Tropea laughs as he recalls Jimmy Maelen's massive impact just nine seconds into the song:

> You know that crashing sound with things falling? Jimmy had a big tray and on it he had loads of stuff, and when it came to that part of the song, he would drop it on the floor. That's how he made that sound and he did it on every take. So after each take, we would have to go over and pick up all his stuff and put it back on the tray. It was the funniest thing, but it was very effective.

Wagner or Hunter plays a subtle melody line over the intro before, at 0:35, the heavier electric guitar riffs kick in.

A choir of voices accompany Alice closely at first – he is in fact, almost part of it. When he does get lines on his own, he sounds a little low in the mix and it lacks the vocal authority you expect such a song to have. Nonetheless, it's a great track, with the guitars giving the riffs a satisfying crunch. It's a good example of how Ezrin's 'kitchen sink' production style can still work well without diluting the guitars. The outro guitar solo (4:37) features a snippet of the riff from 'Wish You Were Here', a nice piece of thematic linking.

Live versions have by necessity been more simple and it works just as well, if not better, in that format. That being said, the album version is rightly considered a classic. Tropea: 'I thought we all played the hell out of that. I'm on the overdrive guitar which is doubled (main riff).'

Allan Schwartzberg concurs: 'I could picture a video of that. It holds up today; it's so strong. I can imagine what it would sound like remastered with all the technology now'.

'You Gotta Dance' (Cooper/Wagner/Ezrin)

Apparently, part of the torment of Hell is being inextricably drawn to disco dance, a theme Alice would return to years later on *Welcome 2 My Nightmare*. Alice uses the top of his register at times, getting a breathless tone that suits the driving disco-tinged music. It shouldn't work, but there's a conviction in the performance from all involved that makes for a satisfying track. The guitar solo at 1:40 being an example of how they manage to get in some edgier guitar without breaking the overall feel of the song. Tropea: 'I doubled the guitar lines (with Dick or Steve), but it's not me on the fills. That's also probably me on the wah-wah'.

'I'm The Coolest' (Cooper/Wagner/Ezrin)

This is almost like a slower 'Some Folks', subdued but still that show-tune style. Henry Winkler was approached to sing the part of the devil, but 'The Fonz' didn't want to be type-cast and passed it up. He was busy anyway with another eight years to run on *Happy Days*. Instead, we get Alice using his deepest voice and the song is no worse for him doing the vocals.

John Tropea notes that: 'I'm on a Small Stone pedal that sounds like an automatic wah. It gives a slow curl on the wah when you step down slowly. In the old days, we used to call effects like those sweetening. Titbits here and there to make a track special'. The pedal first appears at 0:28 and then throughout the song. It's an important subliminal contribution to the song's ambience.

The whole vibe is understated, with everything muted, other than occasional percussion effects, including a bottle being uncorked! Jimmy Maelen does the cool soft-shoe shuffle, and Steve Hunter finds space for a solo, at 1:58, that works well in the low key context of the song. All of this is set around Tony Levin's prominent bass that carries the melody.

'Didn't We Meet' (Cooper/Wagner/Ezrin)

It starts off simply, almost innocuously, but it has a catchy chorus and a tremendous instrumental break from the band. That break first appeared back on the *Nightmare* tour as an introduction to 'Some Folks'. Stunning guitars and insistent percussion from Maelen, dovetailing perfectly with Schwartzberg, makes for one of the most exciting parts on the album. The band get to cut loose and show some teeth.

Alice is terrific on this song, shifting between a softer tone to his rockier mid-range where he gets a nice rough edge to his vocals. At 3:50 the music breaks down and he gets a lovely fragile quality for the final slow choruses that work as a thoughtful postscript. A hugely enjoyable song.

Tropea: 'There's layers of guitar and it's me on overdrive. The guitar volume fills are me too.'

Schwartzberg: 'I enjoyed that song a lot. I got to thank you man for making me go back and listen to that'.

'I Never Cry' (Cooper/Wagner)

This is a well constructed simple tune with a bluesy feel to the music. Alice sounds like he is in the room with you, taking you into his confidence, and it is very touching. Alice has said that the lyrics are an 'alcoholic confession'.

Dick Berg's guest turn on french horn is buried in the mix, but you can pick him out at 2:33 onwards. John Tropea adds, 'That's definitely me playing the hi-string. There are two or three acoustic guitars on the track.'

It was released as the single off the album (backed with 'Go To Hell' in most countries). Having grown up on that glorious run of singles, it was disheartening to find the lead single for the album being another ballad. That being said, this is an excellent song and in many ways, I prefer it to 'Only Women Bleed'. The single got to number twelve in America, but didn't chart in Britain; it seemed a long time since those chart storming singles.

'Give The Kid A Break' (Cooper/Wagner/Ezrin)

A jokey 'fun' song that's another in a show-tune vein – with rewording this would be a seamless fit on the *Grease* soundtrack. There is nice reverb on Alice's voice playing against the backing doo-wop style vocals. Tropea: 'I'm playing on the lines, the 12/8 fills. I'm playing the two and four chicks, the one chick two chick background guitar thing'. Allan Schwartzberg had no problems getting the right vibe for the drums because he was used to moulding his parts to different styles. 'Yeah, that was a '50s style rock 'n' roll thing. I like getting into the different genres; I feel like I'm a character actor like Robert Duvall or something'.

Steve Hunter gets in one of his always-welcome solos and adds some lovely licks on the outro. It's a pleasing pastiche but nothing to get too bothered about.

'Guilty' (Cooper/Wagner/Ezrin)

A rocker at last and it comes as a welcome surprise. There is an effortless exuberant joy to the song that's like a breath of fresh air; the band sound like they are enjoying kicking out and Alice gets a rare chance on the album to use his 'rock' voice. Hearing it makes you wish they had tipped the balance of the album more in favour of songs like this.

Dick Wagner takes the lead solos on this one. His first comes at 0:51 and pushes up the energy levels a few more notches. The bridge at 1:33 – 'bad boy on a summer night' – is effective and nicely cues up the second half. Wagner is on fire, dovetailing around Alice adding some killer licks. John Tropea observes: 'I'm on the rhythm guitar and it's doubled'.

One line from the chorus was used again by Alice for 1982's 'For Britain Only'.

'Wake Me Gently' (Cooper/Wagner/Ezrin)

The intro classical guitar by Dick Wagner is excellent, but it goes downhill from there. Wake me gently – what we need here is an electric shock to raise us out of this torpor. There is a good section, starting at the two-minute mark, a nice chord sequence leading into a fine solo from Dick Wagner.

John Tropea: 'That's me on hi-string and one of the acoustics. I'm also doubling the bass line at times with the acoustic. It's very hard to hear it, but I remember playing it. I remember playing with Hunter very well; he's a great player. A hi-string is a 12 string guitar with the lower strings taken off.'

'Wish You Were Here' (Cooper/Wagner/Ezrin)

Luckily the pulse is about to quicken with easily one of the best songs on the album. A shimmering gong leads into chattering percussion and John Tropea's wah-wah guitar. John: 'I was good at playing the wah-wah. I remember when *Shaft* came out, that's when I bought my first wah-wah. I really felt it. Hunter is on one side and the wah-wah is on the other. At one point I'm playing overdrive too. I'm also part of the ensemble harmony ending.'

Slabs of rhythm guitar anchor the track while the bass and percussion keep things funky. Over it all, Alice delivers a postcard home; a series of frustrated anecdotes about his time in Hell. It builds and swells until at 3:10 Schwartzberg beats the hell out of his kit and the band lock into a scorching hot groove all the way to the outro. Those Schwartzberg fills were truly inspired, as Allan explains. 'Bob couldn't express to me the kind of drum fills he wanted. So he said, 'Come with me, guys take an hour I'm gonna do something with Allan'. There's a limo waiting outside and we go across town to his place. We get to the apartment and he puts on *In The Court Of The Crimson King* off the first King Crimson album. He says, 'listen to these drum fills'. What they were, were like double double-time fills. The tempo was slow and Michael Giles was playing triple the amount of notes, filling in the space and moving it. We went back to the studio and that's what I played'.

The signature guitar riff, and other parts, were recycled by Dick Wagner from the 1972 Ursa Major song 'Stage Door Queen', he and Ezrin guessing that few would spot the lift. Another lift seems to have been made for the verse sections too, which have a strong resemblance to the opening riffs of Rare Earth's 1971 hit single, 'Hey Big Brother'.

'I'm Always Chasing Rainbows' (Harry Carroll/Joseph McCarthy)

This was obviously good fun for everyone involved, but it doesn't wear well, sounding like a pub sing-along. The best thing about this is Jimmy Maelen summoning the bluebird and the crunch in the guitars on the choruses. Tropea: 'That's me and Hunter on overdrive guitars.'

The song is best known for the version by Judy Garland in the film *Ziegfeld Girl*, rainbows being a speciality of hers. Uncredited as a composer is Chopin, whose 'Fantaisie Impromptu' is used in the song's melody.

'Going Home' (Cooper/Wagner/Ezrin)

This is the big ending, with a stunning orchestral arrangement. However, the band are overshadowed by it, the song falling flat under the weight of too much going on in the mix. John Tropea helped score the impressive brass parts for Bob Ezrin.

The chief problem with the song itself is that it just isn't compelling enough. It seems to go on forever too. The line that sticks out is, 'I wonder what happened to Alice?' Indeed.

1977: An Animal Soul Inside That I Gotta Feed

The year opened with Alice working on the film *Sextette,* a dreadful movie which also starred an ailing Mae West.

Reports appeared in January that Mike, Dennis and Neal were in the Record Plant, New York working on their *Battle Axe* album. Also in their band, called Billion Dollar Babies, were former Cooper side-man Bob Dolin and new guitarist Mike Marconi.

Alice's touring band was recalled for a rescheduled tour of Australia/ New Zealand in March. Returning were Dick Wagner, Prakash John and Pentti Glan. Joining them were former Vanilla Fudge keyboard player Mark Stein and Bob Kulick on guitar. The *Nightmare* show was resurrected for the tour, with one addition to the set. 'I Never Cry' had reached number 23 in Australia and it was featured before 'Billion Dollar Babies' in the set-list.

After that tour, it was time for a surprising new direction, which saw Alice taking on the alter-ego of private eye Maurice Escargot, a 1930s Philip Marlowe-type detective. Maurice appeared in the promo videos for the singles, the packaging for the album and in a segment of the show that followed later.

'You And Me' was released in April as the single, while an intriguing contrast came in May with Alice releasing *Lace And Whiskey* at the same time as his former band-mates released *Battle Axe.* The latter was the band album that they had hoped Alice would be collaborating on. Now it had become their début as a separate entity with Michael taking on lead vocals, apart from 'Rock 'N' Roll Radio', on which Neal Smith sang lead. It's a very good album, comparable to *Muscle Of Love,* but you miss Alice. A mastering problem meant thousands of copies of the album had to be returned or recalled. It never got over that setback and the live show they put together to promote the album could only be put on a few times due to the size and cost. The centre-piece was a gladiatorial battle between Michael Bruce and Mike Marconi and was, by all accounts, spectacular. This brief reunion sadly fell apart after these setbacks.

Back to Alice. On 13 June in Century City, Los Angeles, auditions were organised for a new snake for the forthcoming tour – Angel being the lucky winner! The promo push kept going in more usual style the following day when Alice appeared on the *Tonight Show* starring Johnny Carson. He performed *Lace And Whiskey* itself accompanied by four giant chickens with Tommy guns! Prakash John laughs at the memory:

The Alice Cooper tour was the biggest tour of the year, and you get to go on the Johnny Carson Show. The band sits in the orchestra pit with one of the greatest bands of all time – Doc Severinsen's band (which featured Ernie Watts). These were giants of music and you are waiting to play that song where the chickens come out. Before we start the song the commercials are on, and these guys play this wicked minor blues song with the horn section and they are just killing it – they were astounding. And I'm thinking to myself, 'oh God', but the thing is it's a lesson in humility. Don't think you're so great because there's always a time comes along that you will get put in your place. But you know, Severinsen and the band couldn't care less, they weren't judging us. I got to sit in the pit with one of the greatest bands ever, and I got to play the dancing chickens song. But at least nobody saw me.

'The King Of The Silver Screen Tour' commenced with a warm up date in California on 15 June at the Stockton Memorial Civic Auditorium. The band for the tour was Dick Wagner and Steve Hunter (guitars), Prakash John (bass), Pentti Glan (drums) and a new keyboard player, Fred Mandel. Fred recalled how he got the gig: 'I played piano on Dick Wagner's first solo album which we recorded in Toronto in 1977. Bob Ezrin was the producer on this project. Dick asked me if I would be interested in joining Alice's band and going on tour as they needed a new keyboard player. I said I'd be happy to, and we flew to Los Angeles on 20 May 1977 to start rehearsals'. Prakash John also put in a good word for Fred Mandel, who he says is a, 'terrific keyboard player. I got him that gig. I advocated for him to be the keyboard player. He was from Toronto and didn't live far from where I lived. We used to jam together.'

The set-list was: 'King Of The Silver Screen', 'Under My Wheels', 'Billion Dollar Babies', 'I'm Eighteen', 'Sick Things', 'Is It My Body', 'Devil's Food', 'The Black Widow', 'You And Me', 'Only Women Bleed', 'Unfinished Sweet', 'Escape', 'I Love The Dead', 'Go To Hell', 'Wish You Were Here', 'I Never Cry', 'It's Hot Tonight', 'Lace And Whiskey', 'School's Out'. Some songs were edited, and 'Devil's Food' was purely band vocals, while 'King Of The Silver Screen' was instrumental. The Maurice Escargot segment revolved around 'It's Hot Tonight' and 'Lace And Whiskey'. It was a thoughtfully put together set-list covering all the albums from *Love It To Death* onwards, except for *Muscle Of Love*.

While there were high-points, the tour marked a visible deterioration in Alice himself. The concert at Anaheim, on the fourth night, was videotaped and captured a bloated looking Alice way off his best.

The tour was supposed to end in mid-August, but more dates were added, including two in Las Vegas to record a live album. The eventual last night came on the 30 August in Denver, after which Alice checked himself into rehab at the Cornell Medical Center, Westchester, New York. He was still there by November when he got a two-day pass-out to film his part in the *Sgt. Pepper* movie.

The Las Vegas live album, *The Alice Cooper Show*, emerged in late November but couldn't paper over the cracks, looking and sounding like a misguided folly.

Lace And Whiskey *(Warner Bros.)*

Personnel:
Alice Cooper: vocals
Dick Wagner: electric and acoustic guitar, vocals
Steve Hunter: electric guitar
Bob Ezrin: keyboards, piano, synthesiser
Bob Babbitt: bass
Allan Schwartzberg: drums
Jimmy Maelen: percussion
with:
Josef Chirowksi: keyboards
Jim Gordon: drums on 'Road Rats', 'Damned If You Do' and 'You And Me'
Prakash John: bass on 'Road Rats'
Al Kooper: piano on 'Damned If You Do'
Tony Levin: bass on 'Lace And Whiskey', 'Damned If You Do' and 'Ubangi Stomp'
Al MacMillan: piano on 'I Never Wrote Those Songs'
Ernie Watts: saxophone on 'I Never Wrote Those Songs'
Venetta Fields, Julia Tillman and Lorna Willard: backing vocals on 'No More Love At Your Convenience'
Douglas Neslund and the California Boys' Choir: backing vocals on 'My God'
Produced at Soundstage, Toronto; The Record Plant, New York; Electric Lady, New York; RCA Studios Los Angeles, 1976 by Bob Ezrin.
USA release date: 29 April 1977. UK release date: 28 May 1977
Highest chart places: USA: 42, UK: 33
Running time: 41:17

The monochromatic cover design fits Alice's Maurice Escargot private eye film-noir concept, but it isn't attention-grabbing – scattered items on a detective's desk. The better front cover would have been the simpler dynamic inside shot of Alice in character. Warners would likely have felt the image might confuse potential buyers. The packaging is at least consistent and conveys the concept, but that concept doesn't filter out fully into the album. It's there in the opening pair of songs but merely occasional elements of it in some of the others.

Alice's vocals are often low in the mix and he sounds weak at times. Compare his performances here to *Killer* or *Nightmare,* for instance, and you can hear the levels that are missing. Some songs were carried over from the *Goes To Hell* sessions, and 'It's Hot Tonight,' for example, could have worked well on *Hell* with some tweaks. There is a feeling here that this is an album of leftovers and a few new songs. Dick Wagner agreed, telling *Legendary Rock* in 2012: '*Lace and Whiskey* strikes me as being a bit more disjointed. It doesn't have the same continuity as the others'. There are some poor to average tracks, but in spite of that (and the vocal issues), there are a handful of very good songs too.

'It's Hot Tonight' (Cooper/Wagner/Ezrin)

This is a bright start to the album with a strong guitar riff intro. Alice's lyrics evoke a hot night in the city and tie in nicely with the album concept, 'Dogs are barkin', Cats are screamin', Streets are steamin', God's own heat's the devil demon'. It's a rocker, no 'Under My Wheels' as an opener, but it's a good track. Layers of guitars keep things ticking over, and Steve Hunter takes a superb solo. It's easily one of the best songs on the album and one that Allan Schwartzberg remembers simply as 'Just so good'.

'Lace And Whiskey' (Cooper/Wagner/Ezrin)

The album theme is still hanging on here, getting its most overt outing in the lyrics to this quirky and catchy song. Alice gets desperation and frustration into his vocals and the band keep things tight with a sympathetic backing. Jimmy Maelen's percussion touches add delicate flavours to the music which skips along nicely. The chorus hook is irresistible but with lyrics such as 'Be as soft as you can, Put a drink in my hand, I'm as scared as I ever could be' you know there are personal overtones coming through. This will be more even more apparent later on in the running order. It's another one of the best tracks on this record.

Schwartzberg: 'A fun song to play and Wagner is a great song-writer. His songs go to unexpected places. So clever'.

'Road Rats' (Cooper/Wagner/Ezrin)

'(It) is really about the *Nightmare* tour and all the work we were doing, that song says a lot'. (Dick Wagner to *Legendary Rock*, 2012)

There is a real sense of excitement with some killer opening guitar riffs from Wagner, while the band lock into a muscular groove. The solos are all by Steve Hunter who gets in a peach of an extended solo from 3:21 onwards that carries on till the end of the song. Alice sounds inspired too, putting over the vocals with a real authority which is missing on most of the album. It was featured (by Alice) in the 1980 film *Roadie* in a vastly inferior re-recorded version.

'Damned If You Do' (Cooper/Wagner/Ezrin)

A pleasant, inoffensive country and western-style song that comes in, hangs around and little happens. The musicianship is fine, and a big plaudit to Al Kooper for a delightful piano part, but that's about it. You have to ask why they bothered. Surely somebody had something else to bring to the table?

'You And Me' (Cooper/Wagner)

Another ballad but it doesn't hit the levels of 'Only Women Bleed', or 'I Never Cry'. There's an overwhelming saccharine quality that is just too much, especially the hideous instrumental break which should have been edited out. The video for the song had Alice in the role of Maurice Escargot, an attempt to keep the album concept going.

It was released as an edited single, keeping the run of successful ballad singles going. It was backed with 'It's Hot Tonight' and got to number 9 in America, while in Britain it didn't chart.

'King Of The Silver Screen' (Cooper/Wagner/Ezrin)

Schwartzberg: 'That's me counting in. I always went one-two-hey.'

A song of two halves. The first half has Alice, a working man, expounding on his love of the movies and wishing he was a king of the silver screen. There is a clue that a twist is coming when he lists Greta Garbo as one of the stars he would like to be. Following an instrumental break and a tasty guitar solo, we are off into part two. He is 'out' as the queen of the silver screen. Alice declaims over the rising swell of 'The Battle Hymn Of The Republic', a quick nod to *Gone With The Wind* and we are done. It's well played and there is a fun vibe to it, but it could have been better.

'Ubangi Stomp' (Charles Underwood)

Alice does his best Elvis as the band take some time out in the studio for a romp through this rockabilly standard, first recorded by Warren Smith in 1956. While everyone sounds to be having a good time, it just doesn't come over as anything more than filler.

'(No More) Love At Your Convenience' (Cooper/Wagner/Ezrin)

Play it to non-fans and they won't guess it's Alice Cooper, in part because the three backing singers are nearly as loud as him. But this is a wonderfully constructed disco song – odd given Alice's often mentioned hatred of disco. There are countless choruses and a lovely touch when bells tingle as Alice sings, 'I'm telling you tonight's the night'. Indeed it is!

The most comfortable player on this must have been Allan Schwartzberg. 'They credited me with inventing the disco beat, which was on 'Never Can Say Goodbye' by Gloria Gaynor. I was getting calls asking how I did that on the hi-hat'.

Big plaudits to Venetta Fields, Julia Tillman and Lorna Willard who provide the 'wall of sound' backing vocals. All three come with a great pedigree – Fields was an Ikette and also sang with the Stones, Tillman sang with Dusty Springfield and Michael Jackson, while Willard (who is Tillman's sister) sang with Leonard Cohen and David Cassidy. All three have done countless other sessions.

One curious thing is the section from about 1:55 to 2:20 when it drops to just the backing vocalists and music. Allan Schwartzberg observes: 'That's a flat-line and it sounds to me like something was going to be overdubbed there, but it got forgotten about.'

It was released as a single in the UK, backed with 'It's Hot Tonight' and got to number 44. In the USA it was backed with 'I Never Wrote Those Songs'.

'I Never Wrote Those Songs' (Cooper/Wagner/Ezrin)

Another heart-on-sleeve confessional track. It's a quite maudlin song with lyrics that see Alice alluding to his other persona writing 'those songs' that we loved. It is saved by the staggeringly good sax solo by Ernie Watts that makes this track worth listening to. Ernie: 'I was called by Bob Ezrin, who I worked with occasionally, to play a solo on this track. I listened to the part of the track I would play on, which started at the vocal pause, several times. There was no sheet music for the tune, so I created my own part by making a sketch sheet of the harmony. Then I played several takes of the solo section. Bob and I chose the solo that worked best for us, and I think the whole process took about two hours'.

'My God' (Cooper/Wagner/Ezrin)
A brilliant piece of work. Alice literally sings his heart out; you can hear he means this so much. The lyrics are in part from one of his father's sermons. If there is a fault on this it's that Alice is too low in the mix, he needed to be louder to cut through the wall-of-sound production. Instrumentally it's got a cathedral-like cavernous sound as Ezrin gives it everything he can to make this an epic ending.

There's some staggering interplay between Wagner and Hunter, and a couple of outstanding guitar solos that take the track right over the edge. Steve Hunter recalls that 'I decided to start the solo with the melody and just go from there'. And he does, soars and flies off as he has done so often with Alice. It was the last time these two guitar legends would play together on an Alice studio album.

Related Songs
'The Next Time (Next Next)' (Van McCoy)
A dreadful sub-*Saturday Night Fever*-esque disco track, recorded for the film *Sextette* which Alice starred in with Mae West. Alice makes the best of it, while Mae adds interjections. But as the song itself says – next!

'No Time For Tears' (Van McCoy)
Intended for *Sextette* but Mae West cries for no man, so they used 'The Next Time' instead. It was dusted down for the *Life And Crimes* box-set and what we get is a quiet end of the night type ballad. Alice sings it well enough and the arrangement has a piano-led light jazz feel. If you put together a compilation of Alice's ballads, this would be a good left-field choice for it.

The Alice Cooper Show (Warner Bros.)
Personnel:
Alice Cooper: vocals
Dick Wagner: lead guitar, vocals
Steve Hunter: guitar
Fred Mandel: keyboards
Prakash John: bass

Pentti 'Whitey' Glan: drums
Recorded at The Aladdin Hotel, Las Vegas, 19 – 20 August 1977.
Produced by Brian Christian and Bob Ezrin.
USA release date: December 1977. UK release date: December 1977
Highest chart places: USA: 131, UK: -
Running time: 39:38

Alice was going to check into rehab for his alcoholism when Warners
decided they needed a live album. Two shows were booked in Las Vegas
and two lack-lustre recordings duly achieved. From them, this album was
created, not a double-live as was the norm in those days, but a single
highlights album. Alice sounds like he is going through the motions at best,
and it's all rather tepid. The band try hard, but for the most part, it sounds
like music by numbers. The dreadful chart placings (or lack of) tell a tale too.
    Dick Wagner was proud that this was a reasonably bona fide live
recording, telling *Legendary Rock* in 2012 that: 'I may have fixed one or
two guitar parts and Alice fixed up a couple of his vocals.'
    Finally, the cover is a disappointment. Rather than a strong, attention-
grabbing image, we got a montage of different sized pictures of Alice –
highlights of the show in picture form.

'Under My Wheels'
The sound balance is way off, Alice is right up in the mix, but the band
are largely playing in a fog behind him. Occasionally Wagner and Hunter
pop up in the mix, but generally it's all rather laboured. Nowhere near as
exciting and charged as the original studio version.

'I'm Eighteen'
This suffers from the same production woes. When it drops down, it
sounds more effective and there is some dazzling lead playing on show.
What is missing is the intensity, spirit and connection of the original song.

'Only Women Bleed'
Taken at a slightly faster tempo than on the album, the instrumentation,
on the whole, works well because of the less dense arrangement than the
previous tracks. Alice, however, is only adequate. When it comes to the
'black eyes all of the time' section, he stays in the same register. He has
nothing there to get the vocal lift needed to deliver the lyrics with the
feeling they should have.

'Sick Things'

This is a one minute version notable for an annoying distracting keyboard flourish that is intended to add dramatic effect but completely fails. Alice, by contrast, delivers a decent vocal.

'Is It My Body'

Still on familiar territory, Alice digs deep again to get in some of the inflexions and nuances of the studio version, but he sounds uncomfortable on the higher notes. The band turn in a workmanlike performance that doesn't get near the swagger of the original version.

'I Never Cry'

It's clear now that the slower tracks are the most effective. Alice gets into the song well and puts in a good performance, singing happily in his vocal comfort zone. The band deliver good sympathetic instrumental backing, with nice keyboard work from Mandel. 'I did have freedom playing-wise in the live show. I was adding additional passing chords and some country licks to 'I Never Cry' because they seemed to work well with that tune at the time.'

'Billion Dollar Babies'

The drum intro here sounds like it's coming from the next room, which isn't a good start. Hunter and Wagner get their teeth into the guitar parts which keeps things ticking over with some tasty soloing and solid riffing. Alice makes a decent job of the vocals.

'Devil's Food/The Black Widow'

The sound blights this pairing because of the muddy and distant bottom end. Perfunctory cries of 'devil's food' lead into the Vincent Price monologue, an edited version of the original recording. Some nice guitar parts are mixed in with this, but it still means we get part of this single live album given over to a recording of Vincent Price.

There's nothing more of 'Devil's Food' as we segue straight into' The Black Widow'. It follows pretty much the same path as the album version, with Alice finding his best voice so far for one of the album's highlights.

'You And Me'

The Vegas crowd give it a great reception, and Alice is comfortable with the range and tempo. Wagner adds nice harmony vocals that make for a pleasing contrast. In fact, this is a better listen than the album version. The sparser sound is easier on the ears and the song rests on its quality.

'I Love The Dead/Go To Hell/Wish You Were Here'

This is a medley of three, abbreviated songs. 'I Love The Dead' is pedestrian and lacking in dynamics. Prakash John found it surprised him: 'I used to hate 'I Love The Dead' for numerous reasons, lyrically for one. Playing that tune, you sort of have to play all the wrong notes that are in those bass lines, but I tell you it works. Because when you try to improve on the studio version where he's playing a major chord against a minor chord, it sounds silly. So I just had to force myself to play it the way it was, but I liked that challenge.'

Things pick up as we head into an abbreviated 'Go To Hell' which opens with a muscular bass part from Prakash, who enjoyed playing it, 'Because it's very funky. It's very open, but it has a funk sound to it. I enjoyed that one because I could stretch out a little bit'. The band are at home here too and it sounds quite different to the studio version, with Alice on his own for the vocals. It shifts gears into the long outro instrumental break from 'Wish You Were Here', Hunter and Wagner right at home with the duelling guitars. A good medley on the whole that would have been even better if they had been the full songs.

'School's Out'

A distinctly average version of the song. Alice sounds like he is counting down the seconds till he can get off and the slick backing music reduces the original version's snarling power to a whimper.

Archive Releases
Alice Cooper And Friends (video/DVD)

Shot at the Anaheim Stadium in California on the 1977 'King Of The Silver Screen Tour'. The friends in question are the support bands for the day who were The Tubes, Nazareth and Sha Na Na. It's worth watching for the sections with Alice, but it highlights the difficulties he was going through at this time. He looks tired, bloated and going through the motions. The size of the stadium and the gap between him and the crowd is a problem too. He has no audience to directly reach out to. Eight songs are featured and most are the typical selections, only 'Lace And Whiskey' raises a lot of interest as we get to see some of the stage show that had been created.

1978: They've Got This Place Where They've Been Keeping Me

Alice returned to the stage in April with a new tour, 'School's Out For Summer 1978', in effect part two of 'The King Of The Silver Screen Tour' from 1977, being the same set-list and show. However, the band, dubbed The Cornhuskers by Alice, was not the same. Only Fred Mandel on keyboards had been on stage with him before. Joining him were three musicians known for their time with Elton John – Davey Johnstone (guitar), Dee Murray (bass) and Dennis Conway (drums). On second guitar was Jefferson Kewley, who had appeared in sketches for the *Good To See You Again* film.

Alice was in good form after his time in rehab, and having a new band seemed to invigorate him. The band's core knew each other well and this helped them gel together. A good example was the show at Saginaw, Michigan on 10 May. This was recorded (incompletely) for the *King Biscuit Flower Hour* and it's excellent. At some point in the first half of the year, Alice headed into the studio to record his next album, to be called *From The Inside*.

In June the plight of the dilapidated Hollywood sign was in the news. Alice, ever the film buff, offered to pay for one of the 'O's to be refurbished in memory of his late friend Groucho Marx.

August saw him on a flight to London for a date with The Muppets. The music for Alice's tracks had been recorded in Los Angeles, new versions being needed for the show. Alice hadn't been sure about doing *The Muppet Show,* feeling he would have to dilute the Alice character. But on hearing previous guests had included Vincent Price and Christopher Lee he swiftly changed his mind, if they could do it, so could he. The story for the episode was a traditional Faustian pact of Alice offering fame and riches to any Muppet who gave him their souls. 'Welcome To My Nightmare' proved the perfect vehicle for introducing the Halloween-lite story. 'You And Me' with Miss Piggy was an inspired choice, the comedic value off-setting the cloying syrupy tones of the song. For the finale, there could be no other conclusion than 'School's Out'.

From The Inside wrapped in September, with an unusual final recording session. Invites were sent out to 200 guests to come along to United Western Studio in Los Angeles and provide backing vocals on 'Inmates (We're All Crazy)'. Among those present were Cheryl Ladd, Wolfman

Jack, Timothy Leary and Debby Boone. They, along with the other guests, formed The Totally Committed Choir you hear on the track.

A return to Australia had been scheduled for September and October, but the dates were cancelled. 'How You Gonna See Me Now' was released as the single in October keeping the run of hit ballads going.

From The Inside was released in November, with plans underway for a North American tour to promote it that would be the most impressive since 1975.

From The Inside (Warner Bros.)
Personnel:
Alice Cooper: vocals
Dick Wagner: lead guitar, vocals
Davey Johnstone: lead guitar, backing vocals
Steve Lukather: lead guitar
Jay Graydon: guitars and synth programming on 'From The Inside', 'The Quiet Room', 'Serious', 'How You Gonna See Me Now' and 'No Tricks'
Rick Shlosser: drums on 'The Quiet Room', 'Nurse Rozetta', 'Serious', 'How You Gonna See Me Now' and 'No Tricks'
with:
Bill Champlin: backing vocals on most tracks including 'From The Inside'
Sheryl Cooper: backing vocals
Kiki Dee: backing vocals on 'From The Inside'
Flo & Eddie: vocals
David Foster: piano on 'The Quiet Room' and 'How You Gonna See Me Now'
David Hungate: bass on 'The Quiet Room' and 'How You Gonna See Me Now'
Tom Kelly: backing vocals
Jefferson Kewley: guitar
Jim Keltner: percussion on 'From The Inside'
Bobby Kimball: backing vocals
Robbie King: keyboards
Marcy Levy: vocals on 'Millie And Billie'
Fred Mandel: keyboards on 'Millie And Billie'
Dee Murray: bass on 'From The Inside'
Rick Neilsen: guitar on 'Serious'
Kenny Passarelli: bass
John Pierce: bass on 'The Quiet Room' and 'How You Gonna See Me Now'
Steve Porcaro: synthesizer
Michael Ricciardella: drums on 'Serious' and 'For Veronica's Sake'

Lee Sklar: bass on 'The Quiet Room'
Maurice White: vocals on 'The Quiet Room'
Betty Wright: vocals on 'No Tricks'
Produced at Davien Sound Studios, Cherokee Recording Studios, Hollywood
Sound Recorders Inc., Kendun Recorders and Studio 55 in California, 1978 by
David Foster.
USA release date: 17 November 1978. UK release date: 23 December 1978
Highest chart places: USA: 60, UK: 68
Running time: 39:08

This album was set up as a return to form for Alice after his personal
problems, and his sometimes weak previous two albums. The concept
came from the time Alice had spent drying out in hospital.

It saw Alice work with a new producer, David Foster, while co-writing
the lyrics was Bernie Taupin. Dick Wagner returned, but Foster also
brought in his own favourite, Steve Lukather, whose band Toto were
about to break through big. In his autobiography, Lukather recalls:

Foster was producing, but he wasn't a rock-and-roller at all. I was the guy
that cranked up his Les Paul real loud. I was also able to double-track my
parts quick. That wasn't so hard, as I made up my own parts almost all
the time'.

They should have locked the door when Steve was leaving and asked him
to work on ALL the songs! He co-wrote two tracks and was there when
Bernie Taupin brought in the lyrics:

'(He) turned up at Alice's with pages filled with these brilliant, crazy
lyrics, which Foster and Alice managed to edit down. I ended up doing
a lot of the musical stuff on that record and as a piece, it was a very
rewarding, creative experience.

Those lyrics don't entirely work and often neither does the production.
Alice is usually economical with his lyrics, with some exceptions. Here
they could have done with pruning, less Taupin and more Alice; Taupin's
style comes through too strongly. The production is slick but, even with
Steve Lukather's best efforts, lacks bite. Compare the sound and feel of
the similarly incarcerated 'Dwight Fry' on *Love It To Death* to this and we
are a quantum leap away.

147

Joining the rank of guitarists was Davey Johnstone. Alice told *Guitar World* in 2018: 'Davey originally played in Elton John's band, and he was a very sophisticated musician. I'm used to playing with two or three guitarists, but Davey is one of those guys who could probably cover all the bases by himself'. Precisely where Johnstone appears on the album remains unstated. Adding to the guitar roster was Jay Graydon. If his guitar contributions are hard to pick out, you can certainly hear his synthesizer work. Jay: 'I knew the Arp 2600 very well, so that was the instrument used for programming'.

A number of bass players are used and what is clear is that no one bassist dominates the position. Equally, there are a bewildering number of backing vocalists. One who got the call was Chicago singer Bill Champlin. 'I did a lot on that album, but I don't remember which songs I sang on apart from the title track. David Foster produced and I used to work on almost all of his productions. I really had fun with Alice and Bernie'.

An exclusion was Vincent Price, who did record segments for the live show. Presumably, it was felt featuring him on the record would seem like repetition after *Nightmare*.

The cover is another classic from Pacific Eye and Ear, returning for their first since *Nightmare*. It is a gatefold cover that cleverly alludes to *Love It To Death*'s inside portrait. The opening doors reveal a scene inside a clinic, or hospital, waiting area. Ernie Cefalu remembers an entertaining photoshoot: 'We needed a hospital kind of situation and we found a former convent in Boyle Heights, L. A. The convent had been converted into a nursing home with all these nuns running it. So we approached them to let us do a photoshoot in the rec. room there. And they were just so sweet; they were fascinated with Alice. They watched everything and the whole shoot took three or four days'.

'From The Inside' (Cooper/Taupin/Wagner/David Foster)
A great infectious opening track. A bright piano intro gives way to a steady rhythm guitar, bass and drum pattern over which Alice sets the scene. It's clear he is enjoying himself and thriving on working with his new producer and musicians. Foster handles the backing vocals and the strings well, sympathetic touches without swamping the song.

It was released as a single with a significant remix, the guitars being well turned up in a denser mix. The single version can be found on *Life And Crimes*.

'Wish I Were Born In Beverley Hills' (Cooper/Taupin/ Wagner)

A very Elton-esque intro guitar surely means Davey Johnstone is on this track, much of the backing track sounds a lot like an Elton piece. Lyrically it's too verbose, almost too hard to keep up with the information overload.

There is a bright and gutsy instrumental break at 2:25 which features some seriously good work from the band, especially the sizzling percussion track.

It's a good song, but it would have benefited from stronger lead guitar. There is a solo, at 2:50, which sounds like Dick Wagner playing, but it could have done with being mixed higher.

'The Quiet Room' (Cooper/Taupin/Wagner)

'I really enjoy the guitar solo on that song; it's very special to me. I love the piano part at the beginning, which was something David Foster the producer contributed'. (Dick Wagner to *Legendary Rock*, 2012)

Time to slow things down with a reflective song. Adding to the lush arrangement is Earth Wind & Fire's Maurice White, who is the (uncredited) singer behind all the harmony vocals. There's a syrupy feel to it although Jay Graydon gets in one of his synth flourishes at 1:05 to prod things along. You notice that every time he does it on the album things move up a gear. It's the same here and the extra attack and passion are more than welcome. When this song is hitting harder, it makes you realise how much you want more of it on the album. This time Alice doesn't escape and he is left alone, with Maurice White, in the quiet room.

'Nurse Rozetta' (Cooper/Taupin/Foster/Steve Lukather)

Things liven up with the arrival of the titular temptress, and Steve Lukather. Alice's pulse is racing and mine is too because there's a real head of steam in this track with some great twisting riffs. It's also the return of Alice in the kind of form we love him for; he wraps himself around the lyrics and turns in his best vocal yet on the album. Several times he has to hold a long note and he does it admirably, such as 'I can't hold back no mooorrreee'.

At 2:38 Graydon's synth swells and splutters and the song twists into a whole other area. Alice's voice is right up in the mix now, close and personal, accompanied by more minimal instrumentation and it's a great contrast. This is easily one of the album's best songs.

'Millie And Billie' (Cooper/Taupin/Bruce Roberts)

Duetting with Alice is Marcy Levy, later better known as Shakespeare's Sister's Marcella Detroit. Her voice is quite delicate and overshadowed by Alice, who uses his 'conversational' mid-range tones. They aren't a good fit together and the production doesn't help matters with no real dynamics until 2:02. Here things pick up with a big dramatic melody, but that kick-start to the song doesn't last and everything drops down again until the dramatic melody re-appears at the three-minute mark. This time it carries the tune into a curiously underwhelming ending.

'Serious' (Cooper/Taupin/Foster/Lukather)

A breathless fast pace to it, a killer riff and the vocal interplay between Alice and Flo & Eddie on backing vocals is superb. Cheap Trick's Rick Nielsen was brought in to add some of his trademark guitar riffs, linking up with Steve Lukather. Steve's second songwriting contribution joins his first at the top of the pile on this album.

Lyrically it's another pause for thought as Alice muses on when things started to go wrong. The difference here is that he sounds proud of his shortcomings.

This is the best track on the album by a long way and should have been the blueprint for the rest of it. The guitars run riot and aren't drowned in the syrup that affects much of this album. It's a euphoric powerhouse of a song and over all too soon. It should have been a single.

'How You Gonna See Me Now' (Cooper/Taupin/Wagner)

This is the big ballad from the album. It comes over as an autobiographical piece – Alice not just singing in character but also a direct message to Sheryl, written and sung from the heart. Well constructed and beautifully sung, it's a touching piece of work.

At 3:36 a guitar solo comes in, sounding like Dick Wagner's work. It sounds promising for a great outro but rather than let him have his head, the song fades out.

It was released as a single in the UK, backed with 'No Tricks', and got to number 61. In America, it got to the dizzy heights of number twelve!

'For Veronica's Sake' (Cooper/Taupin/Wagner)

Among all of the possible reasons for getting out of the clinic, you might not have thought of concerns for his pet dog. The lyrics actually do a good job of comparing Alice's predicament to that of Veronica, the said dog.

Both are in 'cages', and both are tagged and on medication.

It's a pacey rocker and the upbeat tempo and catchy chorus are well done, but the glossy sheen on the production takes the edges off. You long for things to get messy and dirty. It's a relief, therefore, when the breakdown comes at 2:15 – Alice singing against just the guitars and drums. It sounds less cluttered and more exciting. It's a brief interlude and we are soon back to the gloss through to fade out.

'Jacknife Johnny' (Cooper/Taupin/Wagner)
'(It) was the first song we recorded when we began work on the album'. (Dick Wagner to *Legendary Rock*, 2012)

This should have been the album's big epic. A song about a Vietnam vet and his issues is tailor-made to be a stand-out given a suitable treatment, but it's rather sluggish and the chorus doesn't give the song the big lift it needs to take it to another place. On the plus side, there's some effective backing vocals and the instrumental breaks add sparks with some much-needed guitar.

What we end up with is an average ballad, unusually worked for an Alice ballad, but one nonetheless.

'Inmates (We're All Crazy)' (Cooper/Taupin/Wagner)
The album closes with a big, grandstanding finish. It's pretty good, but Bob Ezrin would have done it better. The orchestral arrangement is excellent, if more overt than we have been used to before. The nursery rhyme chants of 'We're all crazy' are similarly overdone and the song is dangerously close to tipping over the boundaries into something Andrew Lloyd Webber or Lionel Bart would have created.

The pulse picks up at 2:05, the extra energy from the backing choir and the band making a difference. From 3:43 to the end, everything is thrown into the mix for the expected big finish. But it's rather anti-climatic, simply fading away, with not even a solo cameo closing note from Alice. That surely should have been a given to finish it?

Related Songs
'No Tricks' (Cooper/Taupin/Wagner)
This is a powerful duet between Alice and Betty Wright (who had hits with 'Where Is The Love' and 'Shoorah Shoorah'). She gives a gutsy performance as the wife who doubts her man has changed, and Alice rises to the challenge with his best vocals from the sessions. The backing track

doesn't match up to the vocals but is effective enough.

It was released as the B-side of 'How You Gonna See Me Now', making for a mini soap opera spread over both sides of the single! It was probably left off the album because it could only have fitted in (story-wise) if 'How You Gonna See Me Now 'was left off. One of the best songs recorded at the album sessions, and one of the great forgotten Cooper songs.

'All Strapped Up' (Cooper/Fred Mandel)
Written as a piece for the 'Madhouse Rock' stage show. It was shown as a video interlude on the screen so not actually performed live. It's jolly enough with honky-tonk piano from Mandel and lots of guitar. Never officially released in any format, this is the filler it was always intended to be.

'Locked Up Lullaby' (Cooper/Roberts)
This song can be heard played by Bruce Roberts on the *Soundstage* show (January 1979). Including this song would have meant having to lose one of the three ballads which were already certainties to be on the album. It comes over as an earnest self-pitying song and thematically it's in the same area as the much better 'The Quiet Room'.

'Because' (John Lennon/Paul McCartney)
The underwhelming *Sgt. Pepper* film was accompanied by an equally poor soundtrack album. Alice appears with the Bee Gees on this vocal showcase, but shouldn't have bothered. His performance is a misfire as he turns in an unsuitable creepy vocal (at the behest of producer George Martin) that adds nothing at all to the song. Go to the *Life And Crimes* box-set to hear it if you dare.

Archive releases
Live At Saginaw 1978 (CD and vinyl)
Alice's concert on 10 May 1978 at the Wendler Arena in Saginaw was recorded for a radio broadcast. It has been released on many occasions, always with the same incomplete set-list. It's an excellent quality recording from the School's Out For Summer Tour, and infinitely superior to the *Alice Cooper Show* live album recorded five months or so earlier.

The band are red hot; some sources claim Steve Hunter plays on it, but Alice clearly credits Davey Johnstone (along with Jefferson Kewley). Alice is on form too, turning in a better vocal than in 1977 and sounding like he is enjoying himself. One to add to your collection.

1979: Lost On The Road Somewhere

The early part of the year was given over to promoting *From The Inside* and 'How You Gonna See Me Now'. The first promo appearance saw Alice, Bernie and Bruce Roberts appearing on Soundstage in Ontario on 30 January.

The Midnight Special, filmed at Burbank, California and televised in February, was a promo gig in a TV studio for the new album. Alice ran through a seven-song set, featuring four songs off *From The Inside*. A couple of days after transmission Alice went out on the road for 'The Madhouse Rock Tour', the first night being on 11 February at Grand Forks, North Dakota. The band, labelled by Alice as Ultra Latex, were all familiar names: Steve Hunter and Davey Johnstone (guitars), Prakash John (bass), Fred Mandel (keyboards) and Pentti Glan (drums). Alice would introduce Prakash John to the audience as Johnny Stiletto. Prakash: 'He would call me Johnny Stiletto or Johnny The Knife because I was so sharp. I was always a conservative guy. My civilian clothing was not closely aligned to the rock world. Whitey was always Pentti's nickname'.

The set-list was as follows, with one or two exceptions (these being 'Jacknife Johnny' and 'For Veronica's Sake' tried out on a couple of dates): 'From The Inside', 'Serious', 'Nurse Rozetta', 'The Quiet Room', 'I Never Cry', 'Devil's Food', 'Welcome To My Nightmare', 'Billion Dollar Babies', 'Only Women Bleed', 'No More Mr. Nice Guy', 'I'm Eighteen', 'The Black Widow', 'Wish I Were Born In Beverley Hills', 'Dead Babies', 'Ballad Of Dwight Fry', 'All Strapped Up', 'It's Hot Tonight', 'Go To Hell', 'Wish You Were Here', 'How You Gonna See Me Now', 'Inmates (We're All Crazy)', 'School's Out'. Three songs were played as instrumental excerpts ('Devil's Food', 'Black Widow' and 'It's Hot Tonight') and the show featured Vincent Price in three places, including the intro, with specially recorded pieces.

Prakash John was not a 'mover' on-stage, but he couldn't help but be impressed, and learn, from the man next to him.

Davey Johnstone came out to do one of the tours and I learned a lot. In the middle of a song, he would take those positions – the ones they mock in Spinal Tap – but he can do it so naturally, he was amazing. Every night I would look at him, this big tall guy with the big boots on and he played just fantastic too. You are playing a lot of the time these very majestic unison lines, because in those huge arenas with a horrible sound to overcome, there's no time for all the 16th notes. It's got to be big, loud and proud. Your actions have to be exaggerated.

The tour was lavish with eye-popping effects and props, but Alice's lean and wiry appearance gave cause for concern. Also since February, another band had taken flight, as Neal Smith's new outfit The Flying Tigers started gigging around Connecticut.

A tour break in May allowed Alice time to go to Hawaii to start writing material for what would become 1980's *Flush The Fashion*. It became an extended break and around a dozen further tour dates were cancelled, including the New York Palladium and Wembley Arena in London.

The Alice Cooper character was the subject of a Marvel Comics special in August. Marvel supremo Stan Lee had turned down the option of a *Welcome To My Nightmare* special. More acceptable to him was the *From The Inside* scenario, albeit with any references to alcohol dropped!

Alice was back before film cameras in October, recording his part for the movie *Roadie*, which his song 'Road Rats' inspired. He recorded three songs for the soundtrack – 'Under My Wheels', 'Road Rats' and 'Pain'. Backing him on all three were Todd Rundgren's band Utopia. What we have here is an interesting transitional bridge from Alice in the '70s to Alice in the '80s. 'Pain' was to be one of the major new songs, coming as part of the *Flush The Fashion* album with which he would open the 1980s.

Archive Releases
The Strange Case Of Alice Cooper (DVD)
This film was recorded on 9 April 1979 at San Diego, California during The Madhouse Rock Tour. Two songs from the set-list that night are not on the DVD, these being 'All Strapped Up' and 'Dead Babies'. It's a good show with great effects and the band are on excellent form. The *From The Inside* material is all the better for being played live with more zest and attack to it. The hard part of it is Alice himself, who is desperately thin and looks ill (which he was). His vocals are often rushed and he tends to talk through the songs more than sing them.

San Diego 1979 (CD)
Separately to the above DVD, the concert has also appeared on CD. There are many differently titled versions of this on CD, but if it says San Diego 1979 in the credits you will be getting a version of this concert. The sound quality is generally very good on these releases.

Collected Works

The Life And Crimes Of Alice Cooper (CD box set)

Alice and his old band-mates had little to do with picking the featured tracks. Instead, Alice's assistant, Brian 'Renfield' Nelson, put it together with just a few 'you must include that one' hints from Alice. To get a negative out of the way first – no 'Halo Of Flies'! By not including it you can fit in two or three other songs, but that's no excuse. Get past that disappointment and you have a nicely put together package.

The packaging nods to *From The Inside* in concept and there is a good booklet inside with comments from Alice, Mike, Dennis, Neal, Bob Ezrin and Dick Wagner. What attracted the hardcore fans most were the obscure and unreleased tracks spread around the four CDs included.

From The Spiders we get 'Don't Blow Your Mind', 'Hitch Hike' and 'Why Don't You Love Me?' The Nazz's original version of 'Lay Down And Die, Goodbye' continues the pre-Alice Cooper run.

From the *Pretties For You* era, we get a demo of 'Nobody Likes Me' and the inferior studio take of 'Levity Ball'.

From *Love It To Death* we get the single edit of 'Caught In A Dream' and from the *School's Out* demos we get 'Call It Evil'. 'Elected' is featured in its far better single mix. Next on the exclusive list is 'Respect For The Sleepers', which musically became 'Muscle Of Love' with different lyrics.

Heading into Alice's solo years, we get both of his tracks from the 'Flash Fearless' album. The edited single mixes of 'Only Women Bleed' and 'Welcome To My Nightmare' are featured – neither as good as the album versions. Also inessential is the single mix of 'You And Me'.

'No Time For Tears' from the *Sextette* film project is of minor interest, unlike the dire 'Because' from the *Sgt. Pepper* film.

Much better is the single mix of 'From The Inside' with more guitars and oomph. The B-side track 'No Tricks' is also here from the sessions for the same album. You also get selected cuts and rarities from the later solo Alice years, so all in all this is well worth getting, and it's a nice overview of Alice – band and solo.

Old School: 1964 – 1974 (box set)

A lavish celebration for hardcore fans of the Alice Cooper Group. Hardcore because of the three-figure price, which was a lot when it came out in 2011, and hardcore because the content was entirely aimed at collectors. The outer packaging is another school desk, courtesy of Ernie Cefalu, and it's way more substantial than before due to the amount of material inside. For Ernie, it was a labour of love and he spent three months on the design. The band got to inscribe their own initials/messages on the desk lid, and it's pleasing to see Dennis include Cindy and the touching 'R.I.P. GB'. There is a beautifully indulgent book and memorabilia inside, but it's the music and video that is the main selling point.

Two vinyl records are in the set – A repress of the Nazz single and the *Killer In St. Louis* album referenced earlier. This album is also included on CD with the added encore. The double CD set, Treasures One and Two, contain previously unheard and unofficially released, material. Several radio adverts are scattered over these two discs, which add little to your enjoyment, so we will focus on the music.

Treasures One kicks off with 'No Price Tag' by The Spiders, which had inexplicably been left off *Life And Crimes*. Three demos for *Pretties For You* follow – 'Nobody Likes Me', 'On A Train Trip' and 'Reflected'. The most interesting is 'On A Train Trip', which, with some finessing, became 'Sing Low Sweet Cheerio'.

Three live tracks from The Chicago Underground in 1970 are featured – 'Mr And Misdemeanor', 'Fields Of Regret' and 'I'm Eighteen'. All of this show, with the group on the cusp of breakout success, could have been featured. 'Fields Of Regret' is a vast improvement over the studio version, while the eleven-minute version of 'I'm Eighteen' is compelling – this is what Bob Ezrin would have heard and shaped the song we know and love from. A pre-production version of 'I'm Eighteen' follows, which retains some of the original blues feel the song started off with.

Four demo recordings for *Killer* follow, including 'Tornado Warning', which is actually 'Desert Night Storm,' (the early version of 'Desperado'). This time Dennis gets on the song-writing credits! 'Be My Lover' and 'Killer' are not far off the finished versions, leaving 'Halo Of Flies' that has the most to offer. There's no Ezrin, so no Moog synthesiser, and the lyrics still go back to Michael's original words. The rest of the instrumentation is there, and what we get is a full 'live' version from start to finish. Even at this early stage, it's a jaw-dropping track.

'Is It My Body' from Seattle in 1971 closes disc one. Curiously it leaves out the 'Going To The Graveyard' section, fading out just before that should come in, so an odd inclusion.

Treasures Two has the long encore version of 'School's Out' from the 1972 Mar Y Sol Festival in Puerto Rico. Next is the recording sessions for the kids' voices on the studio version of the track. It's interesting to hear Ezrin and Alice getting them to relax and give more attitude in their vocals, but it isn't something to play often. Far better are two songs from the pre-production rehearsals for the *School's Out* album. 'Luney Tune' starts off with scene-setting studio dialogue. Some lyrics are different and it's looser than the released version, with more swing in the melodies and rhythm section. The ending of a run-through of 'My Stars' briefly features, followed by a whole song run through, with Michael playing the keyboards. The lyrics are not the finished item, but the arrangement is nearly there, with Neal's military beats already providing the anchor. The solo and fills are all by Glen and he plays a perfect ascending solo. A demo of 'School's Out' follows, which is similar to the single, but with the rest of the band singing and harmonising the kids' parts.

From the recordings for *Good To See You Again* comes the Madison Square Garden encore of 'Under My Wheels'. Nice vocal interplay with Alice and Michael, and always good to hear Glen burn on the solo.

The demos and rehearsals for *Muscle Of Love* provide three tracks. 'Teenage Lament '74' sounds less dense than the released version. The Latin ending is slower and it sounds like they were originally going to add an outro guitar solo. 'Never Been Sold Before' (as reviewed earlier) is magnificent, riding on a different stinging guitar riff. It's a more direct attitude and feel than the released version. 'Working Up A Sweat' is less urgent and slick than the released version, with almost totally different lyrics apart from the chorus.

The next two tracks are 'pre-production' takes, implying they are closer to the recorded versions than the demos. So it's a surprise that the first track here, 'Muscle Of Love', still has many different lyrics. Musically it's not too far off the released version, with the guitar solos missing. The second track here, 'Teenage Lament '74', is very different. Neal Smith handles lead vocals on what is mostly his song. It sounds less 'fun' than the released version, more 'lament'!

The final track is tantalising – 'Muscle Of Love' recorded at Rio in Brazil on the last night of the band's final tour. It's an excellent quality soundboard recording; you wonder when/if we will ever get the full set released because the band are just killing it.

The package also includes an extensive DVD featuring interviews with Alice, Dennis, Michael, Neal and Bob in assorted combinations. It's fleshed out with video footage, some of which has not been made available before. Although an engrossing watch, it's let down slightly by using edited clips in some places and the amateur camcorder operation during the Alice and Bob interview segments. The interviews are also backed up onto a CD included in the set.

The box set was re-released in a more affordable book style package. Either version is essential for the hardcore fan.

Prime Cuts (DVD)

First appearing in 1990, it summarised the band and Alice's career to that date. The format mixed old and new interviews with promo video and live footage. In 2001 it was reissued with a bonus DVD containing extra footage. The two-disc version is the one to get, as all of the bonus material is worth having. It was well-received in fan circles and remains an essential purchase as it still features material that isn't available elsewhere. Several key players in the story were interviewed, making for a good balance.

Super Duper Alice Cooper (box set)

The central item of this box-set is the film of the story of Alice up until 'The Nightmare Returns' tour in 1986. It focuses on his friendship with Dennis but is let down because Michael is never mentioned and Glen only once or twice. Neal fares slightly better as he is interviewed for it too. This is inexcusable; you cannot shut out his fellow band members, or co-manager of the band Joe Greenberg. There are quality rare films of the band and Alice in the '70s, so it's worth watching, but it should have been far better, more all-encompassing.

The book inside the set features a selection of photographs and memorabilia, some of it rare and never seen before. It's well done and is more inclusive than the film! But it's the bonus features that are the joy for the hardcore fan. The real jewel being a DVD of a *Killer* tour show at Montreal in January 1972. There are problems with the footage; it's not the complete gig and some songs are only partial. Then they had to use audio from other sources to provide the soundtrack. However, it works, despite the occasional synch issues. The video is a high standard for its age, and this footage alone makes it 'super-duper' essential.

Remember The Coop

A partial band reunion came on 10 October 1997 in Houston when Michael, Neal and Glen played on a radio show, and later the same day a full show at the Area 51 club. The latter show was filmed and released on CD and DVD. The connection and spirit between the three of them are clearly evident and it was a huge shock when Glen Buxton passed away only nine days later. In Glen's last interview, with *Just Testing* from 1996, he was asked if he kept in touch with his former band-mates. He replied: 'Pretty much, yeah. Particularly Neal Smith, the drummer – we had a lot in common being from Akron, Ohio and learning how to fight dirty. Mike Bruce – I talk to him. I see Alice and Dennis, yeah'. While his words may not read overly enthusiastic, it's clear in the interview from his body language that he still had strong feelings for his friends.

Neal says that Glen, 'was true grit, the cigarette-smoking bad boy of rock 'n' roll. He made Keith Richards look like a boy scout. His influence and appreciation have rightfully grown over the years'. Fittingly Glen's grave has a tombstone with the musical notation for his intro riff to 'School's Out' on it.

The Sickcon fan convention in Crewe, England on 2 November 2002 was attended by around 350 fans and saw Michael, Dennis and Neal all on-stage together. The evening show remains one of the most life-affirming gigs I have ever seen.

The longed-for reunion of the trio with Alice finally took place and has kept going. Linking up again with Bob Ezrin they reunited for three songs on *Welcome 2 My Nightmare* (2011) and three on *Paranormal* (2017). There has also been a film, live single and album of their performance at The Astroturf, Good Records in Dallas (2018). A bonus live set was also given away with copies of *Old School* bought directly from Alice's website. The four next appeared in the studio together on two tracks on Alice's latest album *Detroit Stories,* which came out in February 2021, again produced by Bob Ezrin.

On stage, the big occasions have been the reunion for their induction into the Rock 'n' Roll Hall Of Fame in 2011, the annual sets at Alice's Christmas Pudding shows, and the UK tour slot on Alice's solo tour of 2017 when it was so good to welcome the band back to Britain.

Dennis smiles and says that:

It's like we're in High School again when we're together. Like getting together with your old friends.

Michael loves the chance to play the old songs again with his friends:

> We get together and it's like we have never been away. It's also about how
> the songs make you feel. The ones that ring my bells are 'I'm Eighteen',
> 'Caught In A Dream', 'Under My Wheels', 'Billion Dollar Babies', 'No More
> Mr. Nice Guy'. Ones that conjure up something inside of me. Those are
> the songs I would tend to speed up playing the guitar on because I was
> so excited to be playing them. They never get old, you know?

Neal comments on what the four share:

> It's like we have come home again, you can see how Alice feels about it
> when we are together. I always thought, 'I hope someday this turns back
> around to being the outrageous band, Alice Cooper, that we created.'

What the band had together back in the day was special and unique. You
don't get that chemistry too often in music or in life, and it is wonderful
that they have got a relationship that works again. The days of outrage
may have gone, but the chemistry is still as potent as it ever was. GB
would be proud of them.

Bibliography

Bruce, M. & James, B., *No More Mr. Nice Guy*
Campion J., *Shout It Out Loud*
Dunaway, D., *Snakes!, Guillotines!, Electric Chairs!*
Gordon, S. *Supermensch*
Greene, B., *Billion Dollar Baby*
Lukather, S., & Rees, P., *The Gospel According To Luke*
Sherman, D., *The Illustrated Collector's Guide To Alice Cooper*
Wagner, D., *Not Only Women Bleed*
Walker, M., *What You Want Is In The Limo* (an overlooked and essential
read)